ACKNOWLEDGMENT

We all have those we can look back through the years of life and give thanks to for their guidance. Guidance's are needed in many areas of our lives. Our Spiritual lives require the most exacting of proper guidance's.

Acknowledgment and thanks for that proper exacting spiritual guidance goes to those of Apple Valley First Baptist Church, in Apple Valley, California.

There, under the pastoral guidance of Pastor Mark Michaels and class leaders, the importance of teaching and learning the unadulterated Word of God was instilled. The strict teaching of the Words of God, unhindered by words of man, has proven to be the correct path to following our Lord Jesus Christ. That instilling has lead to the Love for His Word with a fire, a thirst, of never ending.

Thanks to all so much for that introduction and that leading placing my feet on the proper path. Although many years have now passed and likely many have passed from this world, we know there will be a reunion that will last for all eternity.

Can from time to time hear the words of Harold Childress standing before our class on Sunday mornings, calling out, "how do you eat an elephant," letting that phrase hang in air then saying, "one bit at a time." That is the process we all use in the study of our Bibles.

1

Spirit Revealed Chronology

of

Revelation

His further revealing

Replacing your confusion

Giving you understanding

By

©Love His Word

Author

Donald E. Morecraft

ABOUT THE AUTHOR

Donald E. Morecraft with one of lifes frends Wrinkles

Hope you can tell the difference

Middle of February 2014, a Spirit of our Lord Jesus Christ, placed into my mind the correct chronological path to Revelation. Without that realization a high degree of confusion envelopes the pages of Revelation. That confusion is easily seen in study guides and commentaries involving the book of Revelation. With confusion within teachings, is it any wonder that confusion exists among those being taught and seeking understanding. Understanding is what this writing is all about. Our Lord wants your understanding therefore; his correct path to the understanding of Revelation must be revealed. That path is found in the pages of Revelation. In order for all to gain that understanding, every word of Revelation must be presented without leaving out any chapters, verses, or words as some study guides have done. Our Lord knows what He wants to say to man and He gave all words of Revelation to John to convey to man. Man somehow decides he knows best and presents what man decides will be taught by their study guides. Our Lord is in control of all and all of His words are included in this revealing. We have all heard the phrase, "our Lord works in mysterious ways, His miracles to perform." In the giving of Revelation to John, our Lord embedded His method of finding His path to correct understanding. Clearly, for me this was a real eye opener, like being blown away to see how our Lord worked His wonders. What a humbling experience this has been. It represents concrete proof that our Lord does care and is reaching out to all. No wonder He says, "blessed is the one who reads, and those who hear the words of this prophecy." Certainly He means, every word, nothing left out, all was given to man, thus no filtering of words will be found in this writing, a further revealing.

Clearly, His path given is no accident, this is not a coincidence, and this is the clear path our Lord lay down for you and me to follow. To think that He now is further revealing something that has always been but not realized is more than this person can comprehend. After realizing the existence of His method of revealing, multiple searches were done on the internet to see if knowledge existed among man, of His method of revealing. Absolutely nothing was found. Never has a sermon been heard which included information about His path, no study guide has been read revealing His path. His path has been before the eyes of man for over 1900 years yet not realized. That is the reason now of His further revealing. Did He hide in plain sight for over 1900 years His path to understanding? He assuredly did. Seemingly, for that length of time, He did not intend understanding to be gained although His path was there and man could have gained understanding. Now His path is given further revealing as man requires further help, further revealing in order to understand. Therefore, as the path is already there, nothing new is presented, no itching ear, or new teaching, a further explanation revealing the path is given.

I felt a gentle pushing feeling accompanied with thoughts about the book of Revelation. Our church Sunday School class at the time was studying in the book of John. There had not been any direct involvement with the book of Revelation for a long period of time. At first, due to confusion, an attempt to ignore this gentle pushing feeling was made, however, the feeling returned day after day with persistence. After testing the spirit, the ignoring subsided and the following began by first searching on the internet for the things appearing in my mind. I fully expected to find literally tons of work already done on what my mind hold. Tons of work was found, but, not on the items occupying my mind. That's when the realization set in that perhaps there was more to what was happening than just a passing thing or fancy. Certainly, this was a confusing time concerning these spirit visits. The urge to write was strong so writing began. As thoughts were placed into writings, more thoughts appeared in my mind. The more that was written, the more that was given which lead to an obsession. One manual was completed yet the need to write did not stop. A class was formed and teaching began. Writings continued with never ending events appearing in my mind. For over a year the writings have continued, and now;

Spirit Revealed Chronology of Revelation has emerged.

At no time in my life has the thought entered my mind about publishing a writing. Yet, publishing this writing is the only way seen to reach numbers looking for understanding. The time of revealing to all has arrived. All has not been given for my edification only. He says, "come, be informed, unload your confusion, upload understanding."

CONTACT: 901-410-8130 or donmorecraft@hotmail.com
Donald E. Morecraft

COPYRIGHT PAGE

Table of Contents

PREFACE

From the time of writing over 1900 years ago the condition of confusion has surrounded the book of Revelation. This condition has lead the creative minds of men to inventing **_their_** paths of fulfillment for this scripture instead of seeking its true meaning. There are no shortages of views involving Revelation. Some ministers, because of confusion, tell those in their care, "to just wait and see," rather than teach what our Lord gives a blessing for reading, hearing and keeping the things thereof,

Rev 1:3 *The one who reads this is blessed, and those who hear the words of this prophecy and keep what is written in it are blessed, because the time is near!*
Rev 22:7 *"Look, I am coming quickly! The one who keeps the prophetic words of this book is blessed."*

Such a teaching as just wait and see, comes close to circumventing the instructions of our Lord, the one we are to follow. How would it be possible to follow what is not known because it is not taught? If not taught how would it be possible to follow our Lord Jesus Christ, and receive a blessing? Some would just as soon that the book of Revelation was not part of our Bible, *but, it is*.

It is no accident that II Timothy 3:16-17 is given. Our Lord, all knowing, knew there would be those coming saying, "just wait and see," and those not teaching all His Words given. Yet our Lord says;

HCSB 2Ti 3:16 *All Scripture is inspired by God and is profitable for teaching, for rebuking, for correcting, for training in righteousness,*
HCSB 2Ti 3:17 *so that the man of God may be complete, equipped for every good work.* **Note, it says, (All Scripture.)**

If you're past and present view of the book of Revelation is confusion without understanding, please note; that state no longer needs to exist. A special condition has existed with this scripture writing. That special condition was the will of our Lord Jesus Christ. That special condition involves the inability of man to understand this writing. That condition is attested to by the sheer number of varying methods all claiming to poses the correct path to understanding.

PREFACE

Has this scripture writing been veiled to block understanding? Why for over 1900 years has this condition, misunderstanding, existed? If the other 65 books of the Bible had affects on mankind as the book of Revelation has had, what would be taught and understood today? The same author gave all scriptures, so what is going on with the book of Revelation? Jesus Christ had His reasons for placing a veil on His writing, (the book of Revelation.)

Surly, this should be recognized by most as explaining why there exists the sheer number of differing opinions, surrounding the book of Revelation. Why there exists such a state of confusion. When man does not understand, his mind goes into overdrive and creates. There are hundreds perhaps thousands of differing opinions and _would be paths to Revelation._

Yet we know there is but one opinion and one path that really matters. That one path is the true meaning of this writing as given by our Lord Jesus Christ. Should we, His followers seek that one true path? Will we find that path in the thoughts of man or in God's Word?

Revelation has been veiled for over 1900 years; who is the one that could unveil this writing? If this writing has been veiled, then would it not be necessary for the one veiling to unveil? How would He unveil? How has He provided to man things of His will in the past? Has He not sent individuals in the past to deliver His ways to man? Is He the same today as yesterday? Does He speak to man today or is that just something that happened in yesteryear? Some seem to think He rode like the Lone Ranger in yesteryear, never to ride again. Is He still in control today?

Is it possible that a Spirit from the Lord visited a person giving that person a gentle pushing feeling to get attention, then placing in that person's mind the things of Revelation that He now wants unveiled? Could it be that a person was shown the correct chronology of Revelation and was lead to reveal these things to others? Could it be that you are holding in your hands and now reading the things unveiled and your confusion could forever be removed? Or is this writing just another creation of man, to be added to a huge pile of writings coming from man's creative mind? How can we tell?

PREFACE

Should the proof be in the pudding for all to see? Should we expect to find in His writing of Revelation proof of this unveiling? If that proof exists, that proof would need to be in the earliest manuscripts, having existed for over 1900 years, right before our eyes. There is nothing new found in this unveiling, no itching ear teaching, as we are told will come along in the end times. Yet, there is a further revealing, a further help, to take away the confusion of man by pointing out what has always been. This is not prophecy as that involves something new. This is a further revealing.

Concerning the chronology of Revelation, an example needs to be drawn on; one you can easily check for yourself in just a few minutes time. Please use your Bible, regardless of its version.

Would you expect the one who veiled to place proof of His unveiling for all to see? He did that in the book of Daniel and other books, when He placed chapters out of order. He placed His Words at the beginning of chapters so readers could see. Chapter 7 of Daniel says the 1st year; chapter 8 says the 3rd year, while chapter 5 lists the last year, the last days, the last night of that life.

From His Word's, in Daniel, we can understand that the chapter order is 1, 2, 3, 4, 7, 8, 5, 9, 6, 10, 11, 12 instead of 1, 2, 3, 4, 5, 6, 7, 8, 9, 10, 11, 12. All should now understand that some Bible books are out of chronological order as a *fact* not an *opinion*. The book of Revelation is one of those books. In Revelation He used a different method to reveal proper order. He used <u>word phrases</u> to mark the critical path. Those <u>word phrases</u> have always been there; they have not been added as of late, this will become clearer as we proceed.

For over 1900 years these <u>word phrases</u> have been there yet their purpose missed by man, as they, somehow, were veiled and man could not see the use of or the purpose of these <u>word phrases</u>. This condition was universal; no matter who read, whether a theological graduate student, a minister for fifty years or a person reading for a first time. All failed to see as that was His intension, His knowing. His understanding of His creation, <u>mankind</u> that He could hide in plain sight right before our eyes and we would never

PREFACE

see and understand. Like a missed Easter egg and a child taken by the hand of a parent and shown what was missed.

He now is further revealing what has always been there taking us by the hand and showing His children what we have missed. He hid for His reasons; He now unveils for His reasons.

Explain this veiling and unveiling further this earthly author cannot. However, after accepting what was shown, then reading the unveiling with confusion fleeing, it is a pleasure of sheer delight to gain His understanding, His path to His writing, Revelation. What a blessing, come share that blessing.

Isa 55:8 *"For My thoughts are not your thoughts, and your ways are not My ways." This is the LORD's declaration.*
Isa 55:9 *"For as heaven is higher than earth, so My ways are higher than your ways, and My thoughts than your thoughts.*

No longer should Revelation study guides be printed representing a reading from chapter 1 straight through to chapter 22. Let man present God's Word in His intended ways instead of ways suiting man. He spoke, we should listen, He speaks we should follow.

No longer should some ministers say to those they lead, "just wait and see, the 2nd coming maybe a 1000 years away." Because of a lack of understanding those leading are saying, "just wait and see." Should we His followers skip His writing of Revelation and follow those saying, "just wait and see?" Our Lord has always said, "come, a blessing will be given thy." Just who are we following? When sun light bounces off objects it creates heat and light that we may live and see and without we would have no chance of either. The bouncing affect of reading scriptures should create reasoning and truth, leading to greater spiritual life, as we *absorb* His Words, not confusion and misunderstanding. He has lifted the veil, now reasoning and truth should prevail. Pick up your Bible, turn to Revelation and start the process of understanding. Be lifted to new heights of spiritual life. Accept His further revealing implanting in you His ways, and His thoughts.

Daniel	Jeremiah	Jeremiah	Revelation
1:3-21 605 B.C.	1:1-19 627 B.C.	588 B.C.	1:1-20
2:1-49 604	2:1-4:31	37:1-38:28	2:1-29
3:1-30 598	5:1-6:30	32:1-33:26	3:1-22
4:1-37 565-562	13:1-27	34:1-22	4:1-11
7:1-28 550-549	16:1-17:22	39:1-18	5:1-14
8:1-27 548-547	47:1-48:47	52:1-30	6:1-2
5:1-31 539	609 B.C.	40:1-42:22	7:1-8
9:1-27 538	22:1-17	43:1-44:30	10:1-11
6:1-28 539-538	8:4-9:15	30:1-31:40	11:1-6
10:1-11:35 536	9:22-10:16	586 B.C.	12:1-17
11:36-12:13	26:1-24	Isaiah	13:1-18
Ezekiel	7:1-8:3	6:1-13	6:3-17
1:1-3:15 593	11:1-17	740 B.C.	8:1-6
3:16-4:17	15:10-21	7:1-10:4	15:1-8
5:1-7:27	22:18-23	17:1-14	8:7
8:1-9:11 592	36:1-32	722 B.C.	16:1-2
10:-13:23	605 B.C.	5:1-30	8:8-9
14:-16:63	25:1-38	13:1-16:14	16:3
17:1-19:14	45:1-5	18:1-21:17	8:10-11
20:1-29 591	46:1-28	714-701 B.C.	16:4-7
20:30-22:31	9:16-21	22:1-23:18	8:12-13
23:1-49	598 B.C.	1:1-4:6	16:8-9
24:1-27 583	10:17-25	10:5-12:6	9:1-12
25:1-17	12:7-17	28:1-29	16:10-11
29:1-16 587	19:14-20:18	29:1-32:20	9:13-21
31:1-18 587	22:24-23:8	33:1-37:13	16:12-16
26:1-21 586	49:1-33	37:14-38:22	17:1-18
27:1-28:26	599 B.C.	24:1-27:13	18:1-24
33:21-33 585	14:1-15:9	681 B.C.	14:2-13
34:1-36:38	598-586 B.C.	40:1-42:25	11:7-14
37:1-39:29	18:1-19:13	43:1-46:13	7:9-17
32:1-16 585	24:1-10	47:1-50:11	19:1-10
32:17-33:20	29:1-32	51:-55:13	16:17-21
40:1-27 573	49:34-39	56:1-60:22	11:15-19
40:28-43:27	50:1-46	61:25-65:25	19:11-16
44:1-48:35	595 B.C.	66:1-24	14:14-20
29:17-30:19	51:1-64	642 B.C.	19:17-21
Aug 571	11:18-12:6		14:1
	594 B.C.		20:1-15
	23:9-40		21:1-27
	27:1-28:17		22:1-21
	21:1-14		

INTRODUCTION

The knowledge gained from the above chart reveals that the listed Bible books are all out of chronological order. This information is given to allow you to verify for yourself these facts. Like Thomas would not believe until he put his fingers into Jesus side, you can reach for yourself and gain understanding.

The five Bible books listed are shown with correct chapter and verse placements. Information for the first four books came from the NIV Chronological Bible. Thus this author had nothing to do with the information of these Bible books other than copy and paste. Chapters and verses for the book of Revelation came to this earthly author by way of a gentle pushing, a flooding of his mind with thing of Revelation given by the Spirit of our Lord. That is a serious statements made for serious reasons, knowing full will the consequences of false statements.

What is seen in all five Bible books is a pattern of chapters and verses out of chronological order. Marked by underlining are those chapters and verses. These five books were written over a time span of 800 hundred years. Five earthly authors pinned while one heavenly author gave. To whom should the out of order chapters and verses be credited to, the five earthly authors, or the one heavenly author? Why was the information given in this manner? That information was not shared; this earthly author does not understand that and can only direct you to Isaiah 55:8-9

Today as in the past, most all do not realize that the book of Revelation is out of chronological order. Nor is it realized what affect that condition has on understanding. Our Lord offers a blessing for reading hearing and keeping the things thereof. No blessing can be claimed without understanding. Understanding cannot be had without realizing this misalignment and the realization of the proper reading sequence.

Our Lord equipped the book of Revelation with a path to understanding. That path has somehow been overlooked for over 1900 years. The book of Revelation is the only known book of the Bible to be equipped with word phrases revealing His path to understanding. That path can be known by you.

INTRODUCTION

The common sense, seeing reality, is that chapter misalignment is a *fact* of many Bible prophecy books. Understanding the events of many of these books is not affected to a great degree by this condition. That is not the case with the book of Revelation. Without realization of chapter and verse placements in Revelation; understanding will elude its readers and the blessing offered by this scripture will be missed. No teachings, no study guides failing to understand this misalignment can take away the confusion of those being taught.

Revelation will provide its readers with a blessing as well as making perfect sense when proper placement of chapters and verses is understood. That information could and should be yours.

A *fact* of the past is that the book of Revelation has been taught by many authors and ministers as being in chronological order. On shelves of most church libraries and for sale in Christian bookstores are books following a chronological order for Revelation. This is also taught by well known TV ministers and church ministers. These teachings mislead many instilling confusion instead of understanding.

It is very easy for any person to determine for themselves the *fact* of Bible chronology. The book of Daniel is again used as an example. Turn in your Bible to the book of Daniel and note that in verse 1 of many chapters, a description is given for the time frame of that chapter's events. Looking at chapter 7 verse 1 is listed the events for that chapter as taking place in the 1st year of Belshazzar's reign. Turning to chapter 8 you will read the events of that chapter take place in the 3rd year of Belshazzar's reign. Turn now to chapter 5. Although the 1st verse does not tell the time frame for that chapter and you must read the entire chapter, you will read about the last night of Belshazzar's life. Belshazzar ruled for fourteen years. Clearly, the chapter positions for Daniel, have existed from the time of writing, some 2400-2500 years ago.

Most likely all of us have studied the book of Daniel in the past, perhaps more than one time. Yet it is likely that none of those studies included information about chapters being out of order.

INTRODUCTION

Yet that information is plain to see as that information has always been right before our eyes. That same circumstance has occurred with the book of Revelation.

If you care to follow the chronology in other Bible books you will find a pattern of out of order listings. Why does this happen? We know from II Peter 3:8 that our Lord is not bound by time. Could this somehow affect events being given in a time placement manner? Perhaps, we really do not know the answer.

Suppose that you lost your ability to smell. A walk through a dump would be no different than a walk through a rose garden as far as smell goes. There would no longer be a pleasurable smell distinguishable form an unpleasurable smell. Could this condition be comparable to not being bound by time?

Our Lord Jesus Christ was born as a human taking on a physical body of man why? Certainly, there were reasons, His reasons for leaving His place on the throne of God, not bound by time, taking like a demotion for a while, into our world bound by time.

We find that an explanation is just not within our understanding. What is within our understanding is the *fact* that the condition of out of order of chapters does exist. To claim this condition does not exist is beyond all reason. Yet today many continue to make that claim.

Study guides are continually printed and purchased by church organization that do not contain one word about the *fact* that the book the study guide covers is out of chronological order. Is this done because of a lack of understanding or is this known yet is not taught for a perceived reason? If known and not taught, why? How could this not be known with the book of Daniel?

The condition of out of chronological order for the book of Revelation has been treated by many as if it does not exist. Study guides continually present the book of Revelation as though it is in chapter order. Without this realization and understanding, *you will never understand the events of Revelation* and you will never be able to claim your blessing offered to all

INTRODUCTION

by our Lord Jesus Christ. The book of Revelation being out of chronological order is a *fact, not an opinion.* Thumbing our noses at this condition does not make the condition go away, it causes problems with understanding. As we proceed you will gain understanding and your blessing will be assured

Revelation also dishes out confusion because of the failure of man to adhere to the principles of the Bible. Revelation declares itself to be a book of *prophecy.* That declaration is made 7 times throughout its pages. Found in the following verses; 1:3; 11:6; 19:10; 22:7; 22:10; 22:18; and 22:19.

It is also found twice that the book of Revelation says its words are *faithful and true.*

It is interesting what the Bible says about prophecy and then seeing how man treats prophecy.

2Pe 1:19 *And we have the word of prophecy made more sure; whereunto ye do well that ye take heed, as unto a lamp shining in a dark place, until the day dawn, and the day-star arise in your hearts:*
2Pe 1:20 *knowing this first, that no prophecy of scripture is of private interpretation.*
2Pe 1:21 *For no prophecy ever came by the will of man: but men spake from God, being moved by the Holy Spirit.*
Deu 18:18 *I will raise them up a prophet from among their brethren, like unto thee; and I will put my words in his mouth, and he shall speak unto them all that I shall command him.*
Deu 18:19 *And it shall come to pass, that whosoever will not hearken unto my words which he shall speak in my name, I will require it of him.*
Deu 18:20 *But the prophet, that shall speak a word presumptuously in my name, which I have not commanded him to speak, or that shall speak in the name of other gods, that same prophet shall die.*
Deu 18:21 *And if thou say in thy heart, How shall we know the word which Jehovah hath not spoken?*
Deu 18:22 *when a prophet speaketh in the name of Jehovah, if the thing follow not, nor come to pass, that is the thing which Jehovah hath not*

INTRODUCTION

spoken: the prophet hath spoken it presumptuously, thou shalt not be afraid of him.

In the examination of the above scriptures is man following these scriptures when he is engaged with the book of Revelation, a book of prophecy? By these verses what is man allowed to do with prophecy? Is he allowed to interpret, to spiritualize? Or is man allowed to *absorb*? If man is relegated to *absorbing* why are there so many manmade paths created by the minds of man? Does man really believe the words of the book of Revelation are *faithful and true*?

Should it be clear to us that we are to approach the book of Revelation reading its contents and *absorbing what it has to tell us, remembering that He is the Potter and that we are the clay*?

Following is the reading order for the book of Revelation; with explanations as to why.

Chapter 1

Chapters 1-5 are in their proper order, no special reading or handling of these chapters and verses is needed.

Rev 1:1 The Revelation of Jesus Christ, which God gave him to show unto his servants, even the things which must shortly come to pass: and he sent and signified it by his angel unto his servant John;
Rev 1:2 who bare witness of the word of God, and of the testimony of Jesus Christ, even of all things that he saw.
Rev 1:3 Blessed is he that readeth, and they that hear the words of the prophecy, and keep the things that are written therein: for the time is at hand.

Many continue to be hung-up by the words of verse 3; <u>for the time is at hand</u>. All should realize that our Lord is not bound by time as man is. Peter realized this as in;

II Peter 3:8 *Dear friends, don't let this one thing escape you: With the Lord one day is like a thousand years, and a thousand years like one day.*

The Preterits' View, man's mind working overtime, came from this hang-up, assigning to the time period of 70 A.D., the happenings of Daniel and Revelation. That view is still in the minds of many today although no pages of history support their contentions. Views once formed die hard, no matter the proof or lack thereof.

Rev 1:4 John to the seven churches that are in Asia: Grace to you and peace, from him who is and who was and who is to come; and from the seven Spirits that are before his throne;
Rev 1:5 and from Jesus Christ, who is the faithful witness, the firstborn of the dead, and the ruler of the kings of the earth. Unto him that loveth us, and loosed us from our sins by his blood;

22

Rev 1:6 _and he made us to be a kingdom, to be priests_ unto his God and Father; to him be the glory and the dominion for ever and ever. Amen.

Rev 5:10 _and madest them to be unto our God a kingdom and priests; and they reign upon earth._

Rev 20:6 Blessed and holy is he that hath part in the first resurrection: over these the second death hath no power; _but they shall be priests of God and of Christ, and shall reign with him a thousand years._

A time out is taken here to point out what is listed in chapter 1 verse 6 and found in two other Revelation verses. It should be abundantly clear that the group spoken of in the three verses above is the church group. Further importance of these listings will be seen later.

Rev 1:7 Behold, he cometh with the clouds; and every eye shall see him, and they that pierced him; and all the tribes of the earth shall mourn over him. Even so, Amen.

Verse 7 that reality is here and increasing with every passing day. The smart phone allows the seeing of world events within seconds of a happening. This capability has only existed in the past few years.

Rev 1:8 I am the Alpha and the Omega, saith the Lord God, who is and who was and who is to come, the Almighty.

Rev 1:9 I John, your brother and partaker with you in tribulation and kingdom and patience which are in Jesus, was in the isle that is called Patmos, for the word of God and the testimony of Jesus.

Rev 1:10 I was in the Spirit on the Lord's day, and I heard behind me a great voice, as of a trumpet

Rev 1:11 saying, What thou seest, write in a book and send it to the seven churches: unto Ephesus, and unto Smyrna, and unto Pergamum, and unto Thyatira, and unto Sardis, and unto Philadelphia, and unto Laodicea.

Rev 1:12 And I turned to see the voice that spake with me. And having turned I saw seven golden candlesticks;

Rev 1:13 and in the midst of the candlesticks one like unto a son of man, clothed with a garment down to the foot, and girt about at the breasts with a golden girdle.

Rev 1:14 And his head and his hair were white as white wool, white as snow; and his eyes were as a flame of fire;

Rev 1:15 and his feet like unto burnished brass, as if it had been refined in a furnace; and his voice as the voice of many waters.

Rev 1:16 And he had in his right hand seven stars: and out of his mouth proceeded a sharp two-edged sword: and his countenance was as the sun shineth in his strength.

Rev 1:17 And when I saw him, I fell at his feet as one dead. And he laid his right hand upon me, saying, Fear not; I am the first and the last,

Rev 1:18 and the Living one; and I was dead, and behold, I am alive for evermore, and I have the keys of death and of Hades.

Rev 1:19 Write therefore the things which thou sawest, and the things which are, and the things which shall come to pass hereafter;

Rev 1:20 the mystery of the seven stars which thou sawest in my right hand, and the seven golden candlesticks. The seven stars are the angels of the seven churches: and the seven candlesticks are seven churches.

Chapter 2

Rev 2:1 To the angel of the *church in Ephesus* write: These things saith he that holdeth the seven stars in his right hand, he that walketh in the midst of the seven golden candlesticks:

Rev 2:2 I know thy works, and thy toil and patience, and that thou canst not bear evil men, and didst try them that call themselves apostles, and they are not, and didst find them false;

Rev 2:3 and thou hast patience and didst bear for my name's sake, and hast not grown weary.

Rev 2:4 But I have this against thee, that thou didst leave thy first love.

Rev 2:5 Remember therefore whence thou art fallen, and repent and do the first works; or else I come to thee, and will move thy candlestick out of its place, except thou repent.

Rev 2:6 But this thou hast, that thou hatest the works of the Nicolaitans, which I also hate.

Rev 2:7 He that hath an ear, let him hear what the Spirit saith to the churches. To him that overcometh, to him will I give to eat of the tree of life, which is in the Paradise of God.

Rev 2:8 And to the angel of the *church in Smyrna* write: These things saith the first and the last, who was dead, and lived again:

Rev 2:9 I know thy tribulation, and thy poverty (but thou art rich), and the blasphemy of them that say they are Jews, and they art not, but are a synagogue of Satan.

Rev 2:10 Fear not the things which thou art about to suffer: behold, the devil is about to cast some of you into prison, that ye may be tried; and ye shall have tribulation ten days. Be thou faithful unto death, and I will give thee the crown of life.

Rev 2:11 He that hath an ear, let him hear what the Spirit saith to the churches. He that overcometh shall not be hurt of the second death.

Rev 2:12 And to the angel of the *church in Pergamum* write: These things saith he that hath the sharp two-edged sword:

Rev 2:13 I know where thou dwellest, even where Satan's throne is; and thou holdest fast my name, and didst not deny my faith, even in the days of Antipas my witness, my faithful one, who was killed among you, where Satan dwelleth.

Rev 2:14 But I have a few things against thee, because thou hast there some that hold the teaching of Balaam, who taught Balak to cast a stumblingblock before the children of Israel, to eat things sacrificed to idols, and to commit fornication.

Rev 2:15 So hast thou also some that hold the teaching of the Nicolaitans in like manner.

Rev 2:16 Repent therefore; or else I come to thee quickly, and I will make war against them with the sword of my mouth.

Rev 2:17 He that hath an ear, let him hear what the Spirit saith to the churches. To him that overcometh, to him will I give of the hidden manna, and I will give him a white stone, and upon the stone a new name written, which no one knoweth but he that receiveth it.

Rev 2:18 And to the angel of the church in Thyatira write: These things saith the Son of God, who hath his eyes like a flame of fire, and his feet are like unto burnished brass:

Rev 2:19 I know thy works, and thy love and faith and ministry and patience, and that thy last works are more than the first.

Rev 2:20 But I have this against thee, that thou sufferest the woman Jezebel, who calleth herself a prophetess; and she teacheth and seduceth my servants to commit fornication, and to eat things sacrificed to idols.

Rev 2:21 And I gave her time that she should repent; and she willeth not to repent of her fornication.

Rev 2:22 Behold, I cast her into a bed, and them that commit adultery with her into great tribulation, except they repent of her works.

Rev 2:23 And I will kill her children with death; and all the churches shall know that I am he that searcheth the reins and hearts: and I will give unto each one of you according to your works.

Rev 2:24 But to you I say, to the rest that are in Thyatira, as many as have not this teaching, who know not the deep things of Satan, as they are wont to say; I cast upon you none other burden.

Rev 2:25 Nevertheless that which ye have, hold fast till I come.

Rev 2:26 And he that overcometh, and he that keepeth my works unto the end, to him will I give authority over the nations:

Rev 2:27 and he shall rule them with a rod of iron, as the vessels of the potter are broken to shivers; as I also have received of my Father:

Rev 2:28 and I will give him the morning star.

Rev 2:29 He that hath an ear, let him hear what the Spirit saith to the churches.

Chapter 3

Our Lord makes promises

Rev 3:1 And to the angel of the church in Sardis write: These things saith he that hath the seven Spirits of God, and the seven stars: I know thy works, that thou hast a name that thou livest, and thou art dead.

Rev 3:2 Be thou watchful, and establish the things that remain, which were ready to die: for I have found no works of thine perfected before my God.

Rev 3:3 Remember therefore how thou hast received and didst hear; and keep it, and repent. If therefore thou shalt not watch, I will come as a thief, and thou shalt not know what hour I will come upon thee.

Rev 3:4 But thou hast a few names in Sardis that did not defile their garments: and they shall walk with me in white; for they are worthy.

Rev 3:5 He that overcometh shall thus be arrayed in white garments; and I will in no wise blot his name out of the book of life, and I will confess his name before my Father, and before his angels.

Rev 3:6 He that hath an ear, let him hear what the Spirit saith to the churches.

Rev 3:7 And to the angel of the church in Philadelphia write: These things saith he that is holy, he that is true, he that hath the key of David, he that openeth and none shall shut, and that shutteth and none openeth:

Rev 3:8 I know thy works (behold, I have set before thee a door opened, which none can shut), that thou hast a little power, and didst keep my word, and didst not deny my name.

Verse 8 is a promise by our Lord to open a door. Please note chapter 4 verse 1. Is He speaking of the door to heaven, His heart or are both the same? It is believed in verse 8 our Lord is speaking of an open door into heaven.

Rev 3:9 Behold, I give of the synagogue of Satan, of them that say they are Jews, and they are not, but do lie; behold, I will make them to come and worship before thy feet, and to know that I have loved thee.

Verse 9 is likely those coming before the great white throne judgment seat listed in chapter 20 verse 11.

Rev 3:10 Because thou didst keep the word of my patience, I also will keep thee from the hour of trial, that hour which is to come upon the whole world, to try them that dwell upon the earth.

Verse 10 is a promise by our Lord which must be kept before chapter 6. This promise is the rapture of the church. The book of Revelation does teach a pre-hour of testing rapture, but, does not teach a mid, or post rapture. The hour of trial, most Bible versions say the hour of testing. We will learn that time period is Dan 9:27 a 7 year time period. Please note chapter 5 verses 9 and 10 as the fulfillment of this promise.

Rev 3:11 I come quickly: hold fast that which thou hast, that no one take thy crown.

Verse 11 is another statement by our Lord of coming quickly; however, we know He has not yet made that second coming, while some two thousand years have now passed. The term, I come quickly, does not mean in relationship to a calendar date, but, means the speed in which that event will happen. In the twinkling of an eye.

Rev 3:12 He that overcometh, I will make him a pillar in the temple of my God, and he shall go out thence no more: and I will write upon him the name of my God, and the name of the city of my God, the new Jerusalem, which cometh down out of heaven from my God, and mine own new name.
Rev 3:13 He that hath an ear, let him hear what the Spirit saith to the churches.
Rev 3:14 And to the angel of the church in Laodicea write: These things saith the Amen, the faithful and true witness, the beginning of the creation of God:
Rev 3:15 I know thy works, that thou art neither cold nor hot: I would thou wert cold or hot.
Rev 3:16 So because thou art lukewarm, and neither hot nor cold, I will spew thee out of my mouth.
Rev 3:17 Because thou sayest, I am rich, and have gotten riches, and have need of nothing; and knowest not that thou art the wretched one and miserable and poor and blind and naked:
Rev3:18 I counsel thee to buy of me gold refined by fire, that thou mayest

become rich; and white garments, that thou mayest clothe thyself, and that the shame of thy nakedness be not made manifest; and eyesalve to anoint thine eyes, that thou mayest see.

Rev 3:19 As many as I love, I reprove and chasten: be zealous therefore, and repent.

Rev 3:20 Behold, I stand at the door and knock: if any man hear my voice and open the door, I will come in to him, and will sup with him, and he with me.

Rev 3:21 He that overcometh, I will give to him to sit down with me in my throne, as I also overcame, and sat down with my Father in his throne.

Rev 3:22 He that hath an ear, let him hear what the Spirit saith to the churches.

Chapter 4

Our Lord keeps a promise

Rev 4:1 After these things I saw, and behold, a door opened in heaven, and the first voice that I heard, a voice as of a trumpet speaking with me, one saying, Come up hither, and I will show thee the things which must come to pass hereafter.

Seemingly, chapter 4 verse 1 is the fulfillment of chapter 3 verse 8 the promise our Lord made to open a door. It is pointed out here to John that these events are not past history and have not taken place yet. John through the writing of Revelation is showing us what must come to past. Being history books do not record these things as history happening between 100 A.D. and our present times, we are seeing these events before they take place, which is yet future. What we are seeing is like a program at a super club where a meal is served than a performance given. We are at the point the meal has been severed and soon the performance will begin, and we are reading about the performance ahead of time.

Rev 4:2 Straightway I was in the Spirit: and behold, there was a throne set in heaven, and one sitting upon the throne;
Rev 4:3 and he that sat was to look upon like a jasper stone and a sardius: and there was a rainbow round about the throne, like an emerald to look upon.
Rev 4:4 And round about the throne were four and twenty thrones: and upon the thrones I saw four and twenty elders sitting, arrayed in white garments; and on their heads crowns of gold.

This is the 1ˢᵗ mention of the 24 elders. Some believe this group to be the rapture church group. Please note, the 24 elders have golden crowns. This is important when considering chapter 11 verses 18 and chapter 20:4-6. No other group in heaven have their rewards, their rewards will be given to them during the 1000 year millennial reign on earth.

This group is listed a number of times, (5), in most Bible versions, (6), times in the KJV, as being in heaven and seemingly will mount white horses and follow our Lord back to this present earth at the time of the 2nd coming, which is listed in chapter 19 verses 11-16. Using the KJV, the term, *"four and twenty,"* elders are found 6 times in the New Testament, all 6 times in the book of Revelation, while the term is found 2 times in the Old Testament. If this group represents the church then why is this group not mentioned in other New Testament books as that is where information about the Church is found? It must be said, that this search outcome is very dependent on the Bible version being searched.

Rev 4:5 And out of the throne proceed lightnings and voices and thunders. And there were seven lamps of fire burning before the throne, which are the seven Spirits of God;

The 7 thunders of God are listed again in chapter 10 verse 4. There the 7 thunders spoke; John clearly understands what the thunders say and is about to write it down, when John is instructed not to write their message down. Will we someday be given what the thunders say; for that we will need to. *"just wait and see."*

Rev 4:6 and before the throne, as it were a sea of glass like a crystal; and in the midst of the throne, and round about the throne, *four living creatures* full of eyes before and behind.

The *four living creatures* are found in 11 versus of Revelation when searching the ASV version of the Bible. The KJV uses the term, *"four beasts."*

Rev 4:7 And the first creature was like a lion, and the second creature like a calf, and the third creature had a face as of a man, and the fourth creature was like a flying eagle.
Rev 4:8 And the four living creatures, having each one of them six wings, are full of eyes round about and within: and they have no rest day and night, saying, Holy, holy, holy, is the Lord God, the Almighty, who was and who is and who is to come.
Rev 4:9 And when the living creatures shall give glory and honor and

thanks to him that sitteth on the throne, to him that liveth for ever and ever,
Rev 4:10 the four and twenty elders shall fall down before him that sitteth on the throne, and shall worship him that liveth for ever and ever, and shall cast their crowns before the throne, saying,
Rev 4:11 Worthy art thou, our Lord and our God, to receive the glory and the honor and the power: for thou didst create all things, and because of thy will they were, and were created.

Chapter 5

Our Lord keeps another promise

Rev 5:1 And I saw in the right hand of him that sat on the throne a book written within and on the back, close sealed with seven seals.

Rev 5:2 And I saw a strong angel proclaiming with a great voice, Who is worthy to open the book, and to loose the seals thereof?

Rev 5:3 And no one in the heaven, or on the earth, or under the earth, was able to open the book, or to look thereon.

Rev 5:4 And I wept much, because no one was found worthy to open the book, or to look thereon:

Rev 5:5 and one of the elders saith unto me, Weep not; behold, the Lion that is of the tribe of Judah, the Root of David, hath overcome to open the book and the seven seals thereof.

Rev 5:6 And I saw in the midst of the throne and of the four living creatures, and in the midst of the elders, a Lamb standing, as though it had been slain, having seven horns, and seven eyes, which are the seven Spirits of God, sent forth into all the earth.

Rev 5:7 And he came, and he taketh it out of the right hand of him that sat on the throne.

Rev 5:8 And when he had taken the book, the four living creatures and the four and twenty elders fell down before the Lamb, having each one a harp, and golden bowls full of incense, which are the prayers of the saints.

Rev 5:9 And they sing a new song, saying, Worthy art thou to take the book, and to open the seals thereof: for thou was slain, and didst purchase unto God with thy blood men of every tribe, and tongue, and people, and nation,

Please note the use of different words with different Bible versions. The ASV version is used to list scriptures, for this presentation by this author, as that Bible version is a public domain version. In chapter 5 verses 9 and 10 we see the use of the word, "_men_," and "_them_." The KJV uses the word, "_us_." Research indicates that the word, "_us_," is the more actuate word usage. Therefore, the KJV is also listed to allow a

comparison of Bible verses and to see a clearer rendering of what is meant as a conveyance from God to man.

KJV Rev 5:9 *And they sung a new song, saying, Thou art worthy to take the book, and to open the seals thereof: for thou wast slain, and hast **redeemed** us to God by thy blood out of every kindred, and tongue, and people, and nation;*

In verse 9 we see the word, "redeemed," used to describe an action that is listed in a pasted tense happening. We are told the, "us," came from every kindred, and tongue, and people, and nation. This, "us," came from all over the entire world. The term, "redeemed," is found three times in the book of Revelation. Each time the term is found, it means a taking out of, or taken from. This is seen in the other two occurrences of this term, in chapter 14 verses 3 and 4.

Rev 14:3 *They sang a new song before the throne and before the four living creatures and the elders, but no one could learn the song except the 144,000 who had been **redeemed** from the earth.*
Rev 14:4 *These are the ones not defiled with women, for they have kept their virginity. These are the ones who follow the Lamb wherever He goes. They were **redeemed** from the human race as the firstfruits for God and the Lamb.*

There should be no doubt that the use of the word *redeemed* in chapter 14 verses 3 and 4 is speaking of the 144,000 being taken into the present heaven, or raptured into the present heaven. Therefore, there should be no doubt that the word *redeemed* used in chapter 5 verse 9 means taking out of, or taken from the earth into the present heaven or raptured into the present heaven. In chapter 3 verse 10 our Lord made a promise to take them out of the way. Chapter 5 verses 9 and 10 fulfill that promise.

Rev 5:10 and madest them to be unto our God a kingdom and ***priests***; and they reign upon earth.

Note the word phrase in chapter 5 verse 10, "_priests_." Consider chapter 1 verse 6 and chapter 20 verse 6. These three verses in Revelation all contain the word _priests_. Clearly, in all three verses the group being presented includes the church group. Therefore, not only is the church group seen in chapter 5 verses 9 and 10, the church group is redeemed, (raptured), from the earth from every kindred, and tongue, and people, and nation; before the hour of testing starts.

Rev_1:6 _And hath made us kings and **priests** unto God and his Father; to him be glory and dominion for ever and ever. Amen._

KJV Rev 5:10 **_And hast made _us_ unto our God kings and _priests_: and we shall reign on the earth._**

Rev 20:6 _Blessed and holy is he that hath part in the first resurrection: on such the second death hath no power, but they shall be **priests** of God and of Christ, and shall reign with him a thousand years._

The hour of testing time period mentioned in chapter 3 verse 10, is about to start with the beginning of chapter 6. We must keep in mind that the events of chapter 4 onward are future events, not yet fulfilled. The book of Revelation teaches one rapture of the church group, as a pre-tribulation rapture. Revelation does not teach multiple raptures of the church. However, multiple raptures are listed in Revelation; they involve groups other than the church. Those mentioned in chapter 5 verses 9 and 10 are not those of verse 8. The four living creatures are not human beings and the 24 elders could not be from every kindred, and tongue, and people, and nation; Additionally the fact the twenty four elders are not mentioned in the New Testament yet are mentioned 2 times in the Old Testament, gives support that this group, (the 24 elders), is the group our Lord brought with Him when He ascended into heaven after dying on the cross. There does not exist a clear connection between chapter 5 verses 8, 9, and 10. Saved persons are referred to as Saints. Rev 11 verses 16-18 make a clear distinction between the four and twenty elders and the saints. The saints are to receive rewards, while the 24 elders already have crowns as seen in chapter 4.

Rev 5:11 And I saw, and I heard a voice of many angels round about the throne and the living creatures and the elders; and the number of them was ten thousand times ten thousand, and thousands of thousands;
Rev 5:12 saying with a great voice, Worthy is the Lamb that hath been slain to receive the power, and riches, and wisdom, and might and honor, and glory, and blessing.
Rev 5:13 And every created thing which is in the heaven, and on the earth, and under the earth, and on the sea, and all things are in them, heard I saying, Unto him that sitteth on the throne, and unto the Lamb, be the blessing, and the honor, and the glory, and the dominion, for ever and ever.
Rev 5:14 And the four living creatures said, Amen. And the elders fell down and worshipped.

With the beginning of chapter 6; special reading begins and continues through chapter 19. This is the time period of the hour of trail, the hour testing of chapter 3 verse 10. Many make the mistake of not realizing the out of chronological order of these chapters and continue to list the book of Revelation in a chronological order. This error leads to a condition of non harmonization of scripture verses.

It is necessary to suspend the actions of Revelation for a short while to explain that the book of Revelation cannot be studied as a stand along book. Revelation needs information from other Bible books in order for the person studying Revelation to make heads or tails of Revelation.

That factor is seen in chapter 3 verse 10. In that scripture our Lord makes a promise to take church members out of the way of the hour of testing, some version say temptation, others say trail. Regardless of what your Bible version says, that word phrase is only found one time in the entire Bible. Yet, we as students trying to make since of Revelation need to know the makeup of the hour of testing.

How do we go about finding that information? Do we just start guessing based upon what we have heard in the past? Or do we rely upon the Word of God, Revelation for guidance? We need to know about this hour of testing. What word phrase exists in Revelation that could substitute for hour of testing? Found in two scriptures of

Revelation is the term, "great tribulation." Hour of testing and great tribulation seem to be describing like circumstances. A search for the term, "great tribulation in the entire Bible, reveals three finds. Two in the book of Revelation and one in the book of Matthew. In chapter 24 verse 21 of Matthew, we read,

Mat 24:21 *for then shall be* ***great tribulation****, such as hath not been from the beginning of the world until now, no, nor ever shall be.*

Rev 2:22 *Behold, I cast her into a bed, and them that commit adultery with her into* ***great tribulation****, except they repent of her works.* Rev 7:14 *And I say unto him, My lord, thou knowest. And he said to me, These are they that come of the* ***great tribulation****, and they washed their robes, and made them white in the blood of the Lamb.*

It is easy to see that all three verses containing great tribulation are speaking of the same time period; however, we still do not know what the length of that time period will be, when it will start and what the details of that time period are. Taking a closer look at Mat 24:21 the question arises, "what is it speaking of when it says for then shall be? Reading chapter 24 of Matthew, we find that verse 15 of that chapter is the verse controlling the subject matter of verse 21.

Mat 24:15 *When therefore ye see the abomination of desolation, which was spoken of through Daniel the prophet, standing in the holy place (let him that readeth understand),*

With that finding we understand that when we see the abomination of desolation; spoken of by Daniel the prophet, standing in the holy place, for then shall be great tribulation, such as hath not been from the beginning of the world until now, no nor ever shall be.

A trip to the book of Daniel is in order. Through a word search in the book of Daniel for the word abomination, three verses are found.

Dan 9:27 *And he shall make a firm covenant with many for one week: and in the midst of the week he shall cause the sacrifice and the oblation to cease; and upon the wing of abominations shall come one that maketh desolate; and even unto the full end, and that determined, shall wrath be poured out upon the desolate.*

37

Dan 11:31 *And forces shall stand on his part, and they shall profane the sanctuary, even the fortress, and shall take away the continual burnt-offering, and they shall set up the abomination that maketh desolate.* Dan 12:11 *And from the time that the continual burnt-offering shall be taken away, and the abomination that maketh desolate set up, there shall be a thousand and two hundred and ninety days.*

Again all three verses are speaking of the same time period and that time period is Dan 9:27. A Bible student should recognize that time period as the 70th week of Daniel's prophecy of 70th weeks. We should also realize that each week of that prophecy is a time period of 7 years. We should realize that we have found the time period spoken of in Rev 3:10, the hour of testing.

We should further realize that the verse that sent us to the book of Daniel from the book of Matthew, verse 24:15, will take place in the middle of the 7 years time period. Therefore, we should also realize that the time duration of the great tribulation will be 3-1/2 years, the 2nd 3-1/2 years of the 7 year time period.

Dan 9:27 *And he, (the antichrist, the 7th king), shall make a firm covenant with many, the (Nation of Israel), for one week: (7 years), and in the midst of the week, (after 3-1/2 years), he shall cause the sacrifice and the oblation to cease; and upon the wing of abominations shall come one that maketh desolate; and even unto the full end, and that determined, shall wrath be poured out upon the desolate.*

We now are able to present a simple chart form representing the 70th week. During this time period of 7 years the raptured church will be in the present heaven and will return to this earth with our Lord at the very end of that time period.

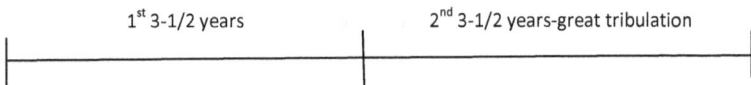

1st 3-1/2 years	2nd 3-1/2 years-great tribulation

The signing of the 7 year covenant agreement and chapter 6 represent the beginning of the 70th week. We should now realize that the hour of testing is Daniel's 70th week a 7 year time period.

In proceeding with a study of the book of Revelation, we soon ran into a condition that has our nose against the wall. We found the description of a time period in chapter 3 verse 10 that was not complete and left us wondering where and how we could find this needed information. That information was not in the book of Revelation. Through a word phrase, "great tribulation," we were shown a path to the book of Matthew. From the book of Matthew our Lord directed us to the book of Daniel. There in Daniel we found the information needed to make heads or tails out of the book of Revelation. Our Lord provided and intended for us to use His path to understanding. Certainly, He wants us to understand, as He says blessed are those who read and hear and keep the things thereof.

Dan 12:13 *But go thou thy way till the end be; for thou shalt rest, and shalt stand in thy lot, at the end of the days.*

There is no sure way of knowing this; yet, it seems that Daniel was shown the things of Revelation some five hundred years before John the apostle was shown the things of Revelation. Yet Daniel was not allowed to write down these things, yet, John was allowed to write about the things of Revelation.

The serious Bible students will need to pay close attention to the order of things given from chapter 6 through chapters 19 as well as to the why that order is followed. We will now proceed with chapter 6 of Revelation.

Chapter 6:1-2

When the 7 year covenant agreement is signed, the 1st seal judgment is broken. Rev 6:1 and 2, the white horse rider

Rev 6:1 And I saw when the Lamb opened one of the seven seals, and I heard one of the four living creatures saying as with a voice of thunder, come.

Rev 6:2 And I saw, and behold, a white horse, and he that sat thereon had a bow; and there was given unto him a crown: and he came forth conquering, and to conquer.

Here is seen a copycat attempt and several more will be seen. Our Lord too will come on a white horse yet He will have many crowns on His head. See Rev 19:12.

What is the content of the 1st seal judgment? Is this our Lord Jesus Christ as some state? No, this is not our Lord Jesus Christ. What is listed are the attributes of the 7th king, known as the antichrist, the person who will sign a 7 year covenant agreement with the Nation of Israel. He of course will wear a crown as he is an earthly king. This is an earthly crown not a heavenly crown. This is a point most miss, chapter 17 explains. When this time arrives a 7 year covenant agreement will be signed. That time may be near. That event starts the countdown to the 7 year hour of trail, listed in Rev 3:10. The hour of tail is the 7 year time period listed in Dan 9:27, the 70th week. The promise made in chapter 3 verse 10, by our Lord, to take the church members out of the way, will be fulfilled before this time. In Daniel's prophecy of seventy weeks, there is a beginning event and an ending event for the time periods making up the 69 weeks. For the 70th week the signing of a covenant agreement is the starting event of that week, while the 2nd coming of our Lord is the ending event of that week.

The 1st seal is the only seal broken at this time, which is the very beginning of the 7 years of the hour of trails, the hour of testing, Dan 9:27, the 70th week. Why is the 1st seal the only seal broken at this time? Because the 2nd seal takes peace from the world and the Nation

of Israel would certainly not sign any agreement involving the existence of wars. The covenant agreement holds for the 1st 3-1/2 years meaning the 2nd seal judgment will not be broken during that time period. During the 1st 3-1/2 years everything will remain a Jewish thing, a very localized thing, like the conditions of 70 A.D. The rest of the world is not yet involved. This time period will be a peaceful time at least for the Nation of Israel. The Jewish peoples will be on cloud nine thinking they have just signed a very sweet deal. The third temple will be under construction, finished and placed into service within the 1st 3-1/2 years of the 7 year time period. Peace will remain for the Nation of Israel until the agreement is broken as given in Dan 9:27.

Note, if the 2nd seal were broken at this time, then Dan 9:27 would not harmonize as that scripture says the signed agreement will hold for the 1st 3-1/2 years. Thus the 2nd seal that takes peace from the world and the 1st half of Dan 9:27 would cause a condition of non-harmonization of scripture. That condition is continually placed into action by those writing commentaries listing Revelation in a chronological order. No circumstance can be visualized in which the Nation of Israel would agree to and sign an agreement including a call for peace being taken from the world. There is a time for the 2nd seal; however, the 1st 3-1/2 years is not that time period. Harmonization of scriptures must be maintained. Scriptures come from the 777 world of God, not the 666 world of man.

During this time period there will be very few if any saved persons on the face of the earth, why? Because the rapture of the church will have just taken place taking all saved persons into the present heaven. There will be many saved during the hour of testing, however, at this time frame perhaps no saved persons will be on earth. The counter of this is the beginning of chapter 20, on this earth and chapter 21 when no unsaved persons will be on this nor the new earth. All wonder is the tribulation time period about to be entered?

Mat 24:36 *But of that day and hour knoweth no one, not even the angels of heaven, neither the Son, but the Father only.*

We are told no one knows the day and hour and although some have foolishly given a day and hour in the past, this author will not tread upon God's Word. We are given in Matthew, Mark and Luke a parable of the fig tree or any tree. From that parable we will not learn the day and hour, but, we can learn to recognize the season in which the conditions will be right for the 2nd coming to occur.

From these listings, Mat 24:32, Mark 13:28, and Luke 21:29, we can know when the times are near. We cannot know the actual time, but, we can know and should know when the times are near. Today the aspects of these conditions are complete or very near completed. What are we speaking of as being completed? Mat 24:4-14; Mark 13:5-13; and Luke 21:8-19. These things will happen before the hour of testing and perhaps within the 1st 3-1/2 years.

Mat 24:15; Mark 13:14; and Luke 21:20 will be happenings taking place in the middle of the 7 year hour of testing. Therefore, the promise made by our Lord in Rev 3:10 to remove the church members before the hour of testing, will have taken place.

To date these things have not happened. We have the assurance of His Word that all things will happen, thus we have the assurance that what has not been fulfilled will be fulfilled. Matthew 5:18 gives us that assurance.

Mat 5:18 *For verily I say unto you, Till heaven and earth pass away, one jot or one tittle shall in no wise pass away from the law, till all things be accomplished.*

The things of Mat 24:16-31; Mark 13:15-27; and Luke21:21-28, will happen as part of the great tribulation the 2nd 3-1/2 year time period which will make up the 7 year hour of testing, listed in Rev 3:10.

If you care; a more full understanding can be gained by the use of a dry erase board used to create charts of events of Revelation. It is suggested that two charts be created. The 1st a chronological chart. That chart will list events taken from Revelation in the order of their numeric listing. That chart would reveal the breaking of all 7 seal judgments, all 7 trumpet judgments in the 1st 3-1/2 year time period which of course would be contrary to what Dan 9:27 says that the signed covenant agreement will hold for 3-1/2 years. That agreement will be broken in the middle of that time period. A 2nd chart should be created depicting the information given in this revealing. From time to time as we proceed, charting times will be given. These times should make up the 2nd chart. A vast difference will be seen, between the 1st and 2nd charts, with much understanding gained.

The 7 year time period should be divided into two 3-1/2 year time periods. The breaking of the 1st seal judgment will take place at the very beginning of the 1st 3-1/2 year time period. That time period will be a peaceful time for the Nation of Israel with the 3rd temple under construction, being finished with animal and grain sacrifices begun. These activities could not be carried out under the conditions of war.

How can we know this?

Daniel 9:27 *says; And he, (7th king), shall make a firm covenant with many, (National of Israel), for one week, (7 years),: and in the midst, (after 3-1/2 years), of the week he shall cause the sacrifice and the oblation to cease; and upon the wing of abominations shall come one that maketh desolate, (defilement of the temple); and even unto the full end, (end of the 2nd 3-1/2 years), and that determined, shall wrath be poured out upon the desolate.*

Clearly stated is the breaking of a firm covenant made for one week, which is 7 years, which will be broken in the midst or middle thereof, at the 3-1/2 year mark of the 7 year time period. This is not a study of Daniel's prophecy of 70 weeks. It is presumed the reader has already gained that knowledge. Please do note that each week of that prophecy occupies a time period of 7 years, which is the bases of the 7 years which has and will be mentioned from time to time assigned to the hour of testing of Rev 3:10.

Several things can be seen from the Nation of Israel's past that would likely be items making up the 7 year covenant agreement. Perhaps you can add items to this list?

1. The right to Israel's existence. This will be an acknowledgement by the 7th king.
2. A peaceful environment free of all hostilities. This would refute the breaking of the 2nd seal judgment at this time.

3. The right to construct the Nation of Israel's lost temple. It is a certainty that a 3rd temple will be constructed.

No suggestion is intended that the three mentioned items would be the totality of the agreement. The 7th king, the antichrist, that will sign such an agreement, would have to be a person in a position of making and keeping the signed agreement. Those requirements mean this person will be a ruler of a country or federation capable of making and keeping this agreement as no person alone could fulfill these requirements. As events unfold we will see that this person will be the ruler of a country possessing nuclear weapons. Why is that assumption made? In order for this person to make war with the Jewish peoples who now live over the entire world; as well as the short time involved; and the amount of carnage which will take place; dictates that nuclear weapons will be used. This is the only known method, processed by man, which could render such results.

We will see that over ½ of the earth's population will die, meaning that amount will be in the range of 3-1/2 to 4 billion people. Truly what our Lord says in

Mat 24:22 *And except those days had been shortened, no flesh would have been saved: but for the elect's sake those days shall be shortened.*

To further explain the conditions for the Nation of Israel at the time of signing the 7 year covenant agreement, there will be a peaceful time of at least 3-1/2 years for the Nation of Israel. A 3rd temple will be completed and placed into service of animal and grain sacrifices. The signed agreement will be between a person that is a king of a propionate country or group of countries. That person will have the power to speak for the entire country or group of countries, meaning this king is likely to be an absolute ruler. The Nation of Israel is very unlikely to sign any agreement with a person or Nation not having the capability to keep the agreement. Thus the agreement will heavily favor the Nation of Israel seemingly giving the Jewish peoples all their desires.

Chapter 7 verses 1 - 8,

Chapter 6 is a holding vessel of six of the seven seal judgments. With the 2nd seal judgment on hold for now, we proceed to chapter 7.

The next event to takes place is the sealing of the 144,000 given in chapter 7 verses 1-8; chapter 7 is the 1st of the split chapters

Rev 7:1 After his I saw four angels standing at the four corners of the earth, holding the four winds of the earth, that no wind should blow on the earth, or on the sea, or upon any tree.
Rev 7:2 And I saw another angel ascend from the sunrising, having the seal of the living God: and he cried with a great voice to the four angels to whom it was given to hurt the earth and the sea,
Rev 7:3 saying, Hurt not the earth, neither the sea, nor the trees, till we shall have sealed the servants of our God on their foreheads.
Rev 7:4 And I heard the number of them that were sealed, a hundred and forty and four thousand, sealed out of every tribe of the children of Israel:
Rev 7:5 Of the tribe of Judah were sealed twelve thousand: Of the tribe of Reuben twelve thousand; Of the tribe of Gad twelve thousand;
Rev 7:6 Of the tribe of Asher twelve thousand; Of the tribe of Naphtali twelve thousand; Of the tribe of Manasseh twelve thousand;
Rev 7:7 Of the tribe of Simeon twelve thousand; Of the tribe of Levi twelve thousand; Of the tribe of Issachar twelve thousand;
Rev 7:8 Of the tribe of Zebulun twelve thousand; Of the tribe of Joseph twelve thousand; Of the tribe of Benjamin were sealed twelve thousand.

From the opening description in chapter 7 verse 1 and 2 we can see that a time is coming of unrest. The reason for that is that the 1st 3-1/2 year time period of the 7 years, hour of testing, is coming to a close and hostilities are about to break out all over the world. The 144,000 are Jewish peoples who have found their way to our Lord Jesus Christ. They are the 1st fruits from the Jewish peoples to accept our Lord Jesus Christ as their Messiah during the 7 year hour of testing. Chapter 7 verses 1-8 tells us about the beginning of the 3-1/2 year tour of duty this group is about to embark upon. Later we will pick up the actions of the 144,000 again in chapter 14 verses 1-5. The 3-1/2 years of service will be the great tribulation years. Seemingly, this group is from the entire world. The forgoing statement cannot be derived or ascertained from the thirteen verses given about this group. This is indicated by chapter 14 verse 3 as it is said "which were redeemed from the earth." If this group was from the Nation of Israel, verse 3 would have said from Israel. This group could be a particle fulfillment of Mat 24:14.This group is not an earthly organization as a certain group claims.

Mat 24:14 *And this gospel of the kingdom shall be preached in the whole world for a testimony unto all the nations; and then shall the end come.*

The words, then shall the end come refer to the 2nd coming.

This group of 144,000 is found listed in two chapters, (chapter 7 and 14). There is a total of thirteen verses, in the entire Bible, with connections to this group, (chapter 7 verses 1-8, and chapter 14 verses 1-5). A search of the entire Bible finds the term, "144,000," in *three verses*. All three verses occur in the book of Revelation, in chapters 7 and 14.

All have likely heard statements made, in Bible studies, as if this group is mentioned in other Bible books or this group is the only remaining Jewish population. I personally have heard that the 144,000 are the one third of the Jewish peoples who will live through the great tribulation and enter directly into the millennial reign. That is a teaching in association with Zec 13:8. Likely, that scripture does have a connection to Revelation, however, that verse cannot be speaking of the 144,000 and we will see why. It is clearly stated in Rev 14:2-5, that this group of 144,000 will be taken into heaven before the 2nd coming and will be before the throne singing a song that they along know the words of the song. This group will not enter directly into the millennial reign. This group will enter the millennial reign the very same way you and I will enter, on the backs of white horses as the armies of heaven, see Rev 19:14.

This example is listed as evidence that teachings are being given with the word of man entered as the Word of God. Well meaning persons and groups have and are presenting things as the Word of God that has origins from man. This is a sickness that needs to be treated by checking everything to be taught with the Word of God before being taught.

This group is a new group of believers. They have come to know Jesus Christ as their Savior and their Messiah since the signing of the 7 year agreement, within the past 3-1/2 years. If they had been believers before the signing before the rapture of the church, they would have been church members now raptured into heaven. This group will likely be responsible for the conversion of a very large number of people all over the entire world before this group is raptured into heaven just before the 2nd coming. We can only presume this group will witness as no supporting scriptures can be sighted stating that they will witness.

Can a time frame be assigned to the events of chapter 7 verses 1-8? _Yes_, that time frame is just prior to the breaking of the 7 year signed agreement. That will occur in the middle of the 7 years, at the very end of the 1st 3-1/2 years. The placement of chapter 7 verses 1-8 will occur before the event of Mat 24:15. A peaceful time is still in existence, but, peace will soon be taken from the entire world. The 144,000 will be sealed not in times of war, but, just before wars consume the entire world.

Examining chapter 7 it is clear that more than one time period is being represented by that chapter. Verses 1-8 represent one time period and subject matter, while verses 9-17 are representing another time period and subject matter. With chapter 7 we have come to the 1st of what is called split chapters. Split chapters have verse groups which represent more than one time period. Chapters 7, 11, 14, and 19 all represent more than one time period. As such; part of a split chapter will appear at one time while other verses will appear at different time period (s). Split chapters are like several chapters in one.

Verses 9-17 do not represent the same time period as verses 1-8, thus those verses will not be listed at this time and will be listed in the time period of their representation. How can it be stated as a certainty that verses 9-17 do not belong at the same time period as verses 1-8? Verses 1-8 will occur before the 2nd 3-1/2 years known as great tribulation, before hostilities break out, while verses 9-17 clearly will take place during the great tribulation as noted in verse 14. Please read again Mat 24:21. For charting purposes we are now at the very end of the 1st 3-1/2 years of the 7 year hour of testing. Your chart should show chapter 6 verses 1 and 2 placed at the beginning of the 1st 3-1/2 years with chapter 7 verses 1-8 placed at the very end of the 1st 3-1/2 years.

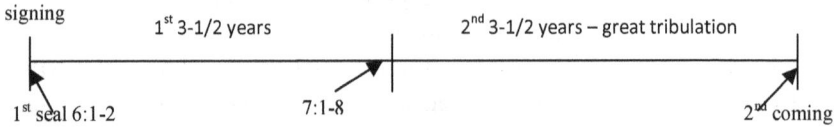

signing

1st 3-1/2 years | 2nd 3-1/2 years – great tribulation

1st seal 6:1-2 | 7:1-8 | 2nd coming

What will happen to the group of 144,000? We find this group again in chapter 14 verses 1-5. In those verses we will see the further activities of the 144,000. These activities will occur late in the 2nd 3-1/2 year time period, therefore, for now our study will place them on hold until that time period is reached.

In a like manner the events of chapter 7 verses 9-17 will occur late in the 2nd 3-1/2 years. Therefore, those events too will for now be placed on hold until that time period is reached. We still cannot revisit chapter 6 for the retrieval of the seal judgments held there. Chapter 8 and 9 are holding vessels for the 7th seal and the trumpet judgments which for now must be passed by.

All the seal and trumpet judgments will have their time placement within the 7 year time frame. Chapter 10 for now will be our next visit.

Chapter 10

Chapter 10 is a complete chapter with no splitting of verses
John takes and eats the little open book;
John is not allowed to write
There will be delay of time no longer;

Rev 10:1 And I saw another strong angel coming down out of heaven, arrayed with a cloud; and the rainbow was upon his head, and his face was as the sun, and his feet as pillars of fire;

Rev 10:2 and he had in his hand a little book open: and he set his right foot upon the sea, and his left upon the earth;

Rev 10:3 and he cried with a great voice, as a lion roareth: and when he cried, the seven thunders uttered their voices.

Rev 10:4 And when the seven thunders uttered their voices, I was about to write: and I heard a voice from heaven saying, Seal up the things which the seven thunders uttered, and write them not.

Rev 10:5 And the angel that I saw standing upon the sea and upon the earth lifted up his right hand to heaven,

Rev 10:6 and sware by him that liveth for ever and ever, who created the heaven and the things that are therein, and the earth and the things that are therein, and the sea and the things that are therein, that there shall be delay no longer:

Rev 10:7 but in the days of the voice of the seventh angel, when he is about to sound, then is finished the mystery of God, according to the good tidings which he declared to his servants the prophets.

Rev 10:8 And the voice which I heard from heaven, I heard it again speaking with me, and saying, Go, take the book which is open in the hand of the angel that standeth upon the sea and upon the earth.

Rev 10:9 And I went unto the angel, saying unto him that he should give me the little book. And he saith unto me, Take it, and eat it up; and it shall make thy belly bitter, but in thy mouth it shall be sweet as honey.

Rev 10:10 And I took the little book out of the angel's hand, and ate it up; and it was in my mouth sweet as honey: and when I had eaten it, my belly was made bitter.

Rev 10:11 And they say unto me, Thou must prophesy again over many peoples and nations and tongues and kings.

It is likely that you have been told that the little book open is the 7 sealed scrolls our Lord took from the hand of our heavenly father listed in chapter 5. However, that is not reality. Why, because at this time period only one of the 7 seals has been broken. That document is still in use and that error is another resulting from a strict chronological treatment of the book of Revelation. By following a strict chronological reading, all 7 seal judgments would be broken in the 1st 3-1/2 year time period, giving a false assumption that the little book is the 7 seal scroll. The little open book is the 7 year covenant agreement. That agreement will have very recently been broken. That contract is now a broken contract agreement no longer in affect. No longer worth the paper it is written on. With that knowledge we can place a time period to this event and the happenings of chapter 10. The events of chapter 10 will take place at the very beginning of the 2nd 3-1/2 year time period, making up the 7 years of the 70th week, the hour of testing, Dan 9:27, at the very beginning of the great tribulation. The event listed in Mat 24:15 will have just taken place.

The strong angel of verse 1 is likely Michael, as Michael is listed as the prince of the Israelites. Yet, we can only guess at that as we are not told the true identity. The word strong is an indication that the angel is Michael as Michael is strong in over powering Satan and his angels in the war of heaven.

Verse 4 is an interesting statement that could indicate a future revealing of the 7 thunders utterance. From the book of Daniel, seemingly, Daniel was allowed to see the things of Revelation hundreds of years before John saw the things of Revelation, however, Daniel was not allowed to write the things of Revelation down, and was told to seal up the words. Now in verse 4, John is told the same thing. John hears clearly the things said by the 7 thunders, which are of course the 7 spirits of God, also seen in chapter 4 verse 5. Will the things said by the 7 thunders be revealed in a future giving? That is the only reason this author can see for the inclusion of verse 4 in the writing of chapter 10. All things are given for a reason. Paul says in II Thes chapter 2 that the restrainer, the Holy Spirit, will be taken out of the world at this time period. Perhaps the 7 thunders are speaking on that subject.

Verse 6 has an interesting segment of that statement which lends to the time placement for the events of chapter 10. Verse 6 is a testament to that time assignment. We read, "there shall be delay no longer." This is a strong indication that the peaceful times have run out, that there will be delay of the great tribulation no longer. Therefore, the events of chapter 10 will take place at the very beginning of the 2nd 3-1/2 year time period, at the beginning of the great tribulation.

While verse 6 tell us that the present time period is at the very beginning of the 2nd 3-1/2 years, verse 7 tell us what will end the 2nd 3-1/2 years. When the 7th angel sounds his trumpet, the mysteries of God's plan will be finished. What this is telling us is that the 7th trumpet will sound immediately before the 2nd coming. This really throws a _monkey wrench_ into the works of a chronological reading of Revelation. Why, because the 7th trumpet is housed in chapter 11 verse 15 while the 2nd coming is housed in chapter 19 verse 11. These verses constitute absolute proof that the book of Revelation is out of chronological order and completely, mystifies this author as to why a continuation of chronological writings continue.

In verses 8-10 John is instructed to take the little open book and eat it. He takes the book from the hand of the strong angel and proceeds to eat the book, which is sweet as honey in his month but bitter in his stomach. This is the feeling the Nation of Israel has at the beginning of the 1st 3-1/2 years when signing a 7 year covenant agreement which they think provides solutions to all their national problems. They believed they had signed a very sweet deal. After the breaking of the agreement at the half way mark, the sweet deal became a very bitter pill with the full realization their sweet deal had gone south. Thus John when eating the little open book had a very sweet taste in his month but a very bitter taste in his stomach.

Verse 11 the closing statement tells John through his earthly writings that the message of Revelation must go out to many peoples and nations and tongues and kings. Thus the book of Revelation has gone out throughout our world for over 1900 years and continues to be the source of information concerning the end of times as the appointed time is on our door steps. Scriptures use both the end times and the appointed time, as a reference to the 2nd coming. This writing is given as a clarification of John's conveyance to man as man over time has managed to introduce confusion almost rendering the message of Revelation to a point of little use. Yet, as seen in chapter 10 verse 11 the message of Revelation is to have an impact upon this world. This clarification is brought by this earthly author through the visits of the Holy Spirit further revealing and clarifying the things of Revelation that have always been there, to continue to have an impact upon this world. Nothing new is presented, no itching ear stuff, just a redirecting to His one path from the many paths man has wondered off onto. May this writing sever to bring the feet of man back to His one path from their many paths?

Chapter 11 verses 1-6

Chapter 11 is another of the split chapter; only the first six verses will be considered at this time period with the remainding verses 7-19 being presented at their appropriate time periods.

Rev 11:1 And there was given me a reed like unto a rod: and one said, Rise, and measure the temple of God, and the altar, and them that worship therein.

Rev 11:2 And the court which is without the temple leave without, and measure it not; for it hath been given unto the nations: and the holy city shall they tread under foot forty and two months

Rev 11:3 And I will give unto my two witnesses, and they shall prophesy a thousand two hundred and threescore days, clothed in sackcloth.

Rev 11:4 These are the two olive trees and the two candlesticks, standing before the Lord of the earth.

Rev 11:5 And if any man desireth to hurt them, fire proceedeth out of their mouth and devoureth their enemies; and if any man shall desire to hurt them, in this manner must he be killed.

Rev 11:6 These have the power to shut the heaven, that it rain not during the days of their prophecy: and they have power over the waters to turn them into blood, and to smite the earth with every plague, as often as they shall desire.

Verses 1 and 2 present proof that a 3rd temple will be constructed. These verses also tells that the temple complex will be taken over by persons other than Jewish descendants and we are given the amount of time the complex will undergo this intrusion. This is a clear sign of aggression as non Jewish persons are not allowed on the temple properties. Verses 1 and 2 fit very well with Dan 9:27 which says the agreement will be broken in the middle of the week, in the middle of the 7 year 70th week. That is the time frame for charting of chapter 11 verses 1-6. Chapter 10 and chapter 11 verses 1-6 will occupy the same charting space. That charting should be placed at the very beginning of the 2nd 3-1/2 years.

Likely, Ezekiel chapters 40-48 are listing information about the third temple, which will be built and finished before the 2nd 3-1/2 years begin.

Now we consider the second event of verses 1-6. Two witnesses listed in verses 3-6 will prophecy unto the Nation of Israel dressed in sackcloth. They will be allowed to protect themselves with fire coming from their months.

In verse 4 is a description of the Holy of Holies of the defiled 3rd temple, which has been taken over by Satan and the beast and turned into their office space. Seemingly, the two witnesses will go into the Holy of Holies and prophecy directly to Satan and the beast. This same bravery was seen in Egypt when Moses prophesied before pharaoh. Wood carvings on the walls of the temple is a known fact. The olive trees could be wall carvings. The lamp stands are items found as furniture in the Holy of Holies.

These two witnesses are given powers to stop rain fall, to turn water into blood, and to bring plagues upon the earth as offend as they wish. These powers and their affects are seen in both the trumpet and bowl judgments and this is very suggestive that the two witnesses play a major part in the administration of the trumpet and bowl judgments.

The work of the two witnesses will continue throughout all of the great tribulation time period culminating with them been killed, life breath into their dead bodies, and they are called, raptured, into the present heaven.

We see the amazing work of our Lord Jesus Christ. The Nation of Israel who has turned their backs upon Jesus Christ their Savior and Messiah, has just had the chair kicked out from under them with the breaking of the 7 year agreement, and their Messiah, which most do not yet except, steps forward to send them witnesses to provide the good news which undoubtedly well result in a great many accepting Jesus Christ as their Savior and Messiah. Israel turned their backs yet Jesus remained true to His chosen people.

These two witnesses will witness to the Nation of Israel from the City of Jerusalem for a time period of 1260 days. Of course the 42 months and the 1260 days listed in verses 2 and 3 equals a time period of 3-1/2 years. The same 3-1/2 years our Lord calls the great tribulation. Much confusion has centered on the time of service of these two witnesses. That confusion is caused by the following of a strict chronological reading of Revelation, with those making that error thinking these two witnesses will witness in the 1st 3-1/2 years. Charting will reveal this problem. Many assign names to these two witnesses; however, no clear scripture path is given to the identity of these individuals. Moses and Elijah did possess powers like those of the two witnesses and that is the reasons the two witnesses are thought to be those two men.

We know the beginning event of the 2nd 3-1/2 years and we know the ending event of this time period. Chapter 11 is the clearest example of a split chapter as exact times are listed in verses 2 and 3. Verses 1-6 represent a time period starting just after the breaking of the 7 year covenant agreement. Verses 7-19 represent a time period 3-1/2 years after the breaking of the agreement. That time period is the very end of the great tribulation, the 2nd coming culminates that time period. Therefore, verses 7-19 will be placed just before the 2nd coming. Of course verses 7-19 will not be listed here, but, will be listed in their rightful time period. That time period satisfies all scriptures speaking about the 7th trumpet sounding just before the 2nd coming. We should be realizing that the book of Revelation is much more revealing about the time placement of events than most realized.

Chapter 12

Satan kicked out of heaven or is he still there?
Chapter 12 is a very confused scripture due to the lack of man to pay attention to what is presented.
Woe to the earth and the sea
He knows he has but a short time

From chapter 4 all of Revelation is a continuance of John being called into heaven. John see all events from that vantage point. That is why the designation in verses 1 and 3 says, *"a sign in heaven."* John is shown things which have already happened that are relevant to things that have not yet happened, with the dividing line between verses 5 and 6.

Rev 12:1 And a great sign was seen in heaven: a woman arrayed with the sun, and the moon under her feet, and upon her head a crown of twelve stars;

Rev 12:2 and she was with child; and she crieth out, travailing in birth, and in pain to be delivered.

Rev 12:3 And there was seen another sign in heaven: and behold, a great red dragon, having seven heads and ten horns, and upon his heads seven diadems.

Rev 12:4 [1st]And his tail draweth the third part of the stars of heaven, and did cast them to the earth:[2nd] and the dragon standeth before the woman that is about to be delivered, that when she is delivered he may devour her child.

Rev 12:5[1st] And she was delivered of a son,[2nd] a man child, who is to rule all the nations with a rod of iron:[3rd] and her child was caught up unto God, and unto his throne.

Dividing Line

$$\longleftrightarrow$$

Rev 12:6 *And the woman fled into the wilderness, where she hath a place prepared of God, that there they may nourish her a thousand two hundred and threescore days.*

Rev 12:7 And there was war in heaven: Michael and his angels going forth to war with the dragon; and the dragon warred and his angels;

Rev 12:8 And they prevailed not, neither was their place found any more in heaven.

Rev 12:9 And the great dragon was cast down, the old serpent, he that is called the Devil and Satan, the deceiver of the whole world; he was cast down to the earth, and his angels were cast down with him.

Rev 12:10 And I heard a great voice in heaven, saying, Now is come the salvation, and the power, and the kingdom of our God, and the authority of his Christ: for the accuser of our brethren is cast down, who accuseth them before our God day and night.

Rev 12:11 And they overcame him because of the blood of the Lamb, and because of the word of their testimony; and they loved not their life even unto death.

Rev 12:12 Therefore rejoice, O heavens, and ye that dwell in them. Woe for the earth and for the sea: because the devil is gone down unto you, having great wrath, knowing that he hath but a short time.

It is hard for us to understand why Satan was ever allowed access into heaven. Yet, we know Satan has been given that privilege. From verse 3 we see that Satan still has that privilege at the time our Lord is born. We can read about his heavenly access in the book of Job. We can see that access still existed at the time of our Lord's earthly birth. What did or will happen to that privilege? What did or will Satan do to have that privilege taken away?

Isa 14:12 Shining morning star, how you have fallen from the heavens! You destroyer of nations, you have been cut down to the ground.
Isa 14:13 You said to yourself: "I will ascend to the heavens; I will set up my throne above the stars of God. I will sit on the mount of the gods' assembly, in the remotest parts of the North.
Isa 14:14 I will ascend above the highest clouds; I will make myself like the Most High."

Did or will Satan try to take over heaven? Did or will Satan try to take over the throne room in heaven? Did or will Satan try to enter the Holy of Holies in heaven and set on the throne of God? No concrete connection is given; yet, scriptures listed in the book of Isaiah seem to

fit the occasion of Satan crossing the line and being kicked out of heaven.

Chapter 12 verse 12 signals for us what is the cause of the great tribulation. Satan being kicked out of heaven causes the conditions of that time period coming upon the earth. Verse 12 says Woe to the earth and the sea. Have you ever read the 7 seal judgments, the 7 trumpet and 7 bowl judgments? Those events take place during the great tribulation, and that time period will start the very instance Satan is kicked out of heaven. Has that time period occurred? Some say so? Some are just misinformed when making such statements, as the conditions of the great tribulation have not ever been known. Thus Satan is still in heaven.

Seems Satan will try to take over heaven itself and of course will fail at that attempt, yet, Mat 24:15 along with Dan 9:27, reveals that Satan will be successful at taking over the earthly temple. What Satan could not do in heaven, he, for a short time of 3-1/2 years, will do on earth. That time period is called by our Lord great tribulation. Chapter 13 gives us a look at those times.

Mat 24:21 *For at that time there will be great tribulation, the kind that hasn't taken place from the beginning of the world until now and never will again!*
Mat 24:22 *Unless those days were limited, no one would survive. But those days will be limited because of the elect.*

Why will there be a great tribulation and that condition will never again happen? Because Satan will never again be allowed into heaven and can never again be kicked out of heaven. Thus another great tribulation will never again happen.

Rev 12:13 And when the dragon saw that he was cast down to the earth, he persecuted the woman that brought forth the man child.
Rev 12:14 *And there were given to the woman the two wings of the great eagle, that she might fly into the wilderness unto her place, where she is nourished for a time, and times, and half a time, from the face of the serpent.*
Rev 12:15 And the serpent cast out of his mouth after the woman water as

58

a river, that he might cause her to be carried away by the stream. Rev 12:16 And the earth helped the woman, and the earth opened her mouth and swallowed up the river which the dragon cast out of his mouth. Rev 12:17 And the dragon waxed wroth with the woman, and went away to make war with the rest of her seed, that keep the commandments of God, and hold the testimony of Jesus:

Chapter 12 is a heavenly scene. Verses 1-4 give an account of the birth of our Lord Jesus Christ by the woman which of course is the Nation of Israel as Mary was of Jewish descent and as the Jewish peoples are His chosen people. Verses 1-4 are given like a review to bring us up to date on the presented subject matter which is the kicking out of heaven of Satan. Verses 4 and 5 are what are known as time gaps. Time gaps are not unusual in the Bible. Isaiah 9:6 is a popular time gap known to all.

Isa 9:6 *1stFor unto us a child is born, 2nd unto us a son is given; 3rd and the government shall be upon his shoulder: 4th and his name shall be called Wonderful, Counsellor, Mighty God, Everlasting Father, Prince of Peace.*

In chapter 12 verse 4 is seen both a future and past event. Time gaps can jump either forward or backward in time. The 1st part of verse 4 jumps forward to the time of verses 7, 8, and 9. That is a jump in time of over 2000 years and counting. The 2nd part jumps backward in time as Satan did try to kill the Christ Child, through the actions of King Herod. Remember John is seeing these events around 95 A.D. Satan's angels will be cast to earth, as listed in verses 7, 8, and 9, yet a future event, while Satan did attempt to kill the Christ child when born 2000 years age a past event. In chapter 12 verse 5 is seen three time periods separated by comas. The 1st time gap represents 4-6 B.C. the time of the birth of Jesus Christ to Mary. The 2nd time gap represents the millennial reign which of course is yet to happen and the 3rd time gap represents around 30 A.D. when Jesus ascended into heaven after dying on the cross. Time gaps are not unlike our conversations with others; when we may speak of a different time period with every breath we take and in doing so sometimes lose those we are talking to.

Verse 6 is like a road sign meant to get our attention and to inform us. Verse 6 should be compared with verse 14 as both verses give the same

information. Both verses tell about a time when the woman, the Nation of Israel will flee from the presence of Satan; that time is yet future. Both verses give us a time designation equaling 3-1/2 years. Why then is verse 6 given if verse 6 lists the same information as verse 14? Verse 6 is given to alert us to a time change taking place; it is a dividing line between the past and the future in chapter 12. Verse 6 is meant to stop confusion over when the war will take place in heaven listed in verses 7, 8, and 9. Verse 6 tells of a future event, the time of the great tribulation, just as verse 14 speaks of a future event, the time of the great tribulation. This should lead to the knowledge that verses 7, 8 and 9 are also future events as the great tribulation is a future event. Yet today much confusion exists as many think Satan has already been kicked out of heaven. That is mentally drawn because of the lack of attention to what is being presented to man in the verses of chapter 12. That same lack of attention throughout Revelation has lead to many misunderstandings, many invented paths.

How can we be sure chapter 12 verse 6 is speaking of the future? Because of the listing of 1260 days which equals 3-1/2 years. No place in history is there an account of such a time period. We know that His Words will come true 100%, therefore, as this time period is not history, and cannot be found in the past; it is a future time period.

Just ask a number of people this question and you will understand more fully the meaning of verse 6. Ask; "when was Satan kicked out of heaven?" You are likely to receive an answer like this. "Well I don't know the exact time but it was a long time ago." You could use the opportunity as an open door to witness and reduce their confusion as you will be armed with understanding.

In actuality, Satan has not been kicked out of heaven, he is still there. What chapter 12 is telling us is that Satan and his angels will one day in the future be kicked out of heaven; however, that day has not yet arrived. If verse 6 was recognized as a future event, which it is, then the war in heaven resulting in Satan being kicked out of heaven would also be recognized as being yet future. That is the reason that verses 6 and 14 convey the same message. Highway signs are missed, or ignored so has been verse 6. Verses 6 and 14 are supposed to have a recognizable connection. A study guide further compounds this confusion as on page 7 of that guide for a daily reading is listed verses 1-6, when that listing should be 1-5, then 6-14. Confusion is introduced as the dividing line is crossed without realizing it is there.

We have an advocate our Lord Jesus Christ who is our high priest representing us before the Heavenly Father as Satan is continually accusing us before the throne of God. With the above in mind that Satan is still in heaven today accusing believer's before the throne of God, verse 12 takes on a whole new meaning, when saying, "knowing that he hath but a short time." Truly, Satan will have but a short time of 3-1/2 years to work his self set magic trying to take over the universe, when he is _kicked out of heaven_ as a future event.

1Jn_2:1 *My little children, these things write I unto you that ye may not sin. And if any man sin, we have an Advocate with the Father, Jesus Christ the righteous:*

Why is it necessary for Jesus Christ to be our Advocate before the heavenly throne, the heavenly Father if Satan has already been kicked out of heaven? If Satan has already been kicked out of heaven, how long is the short time he has and when will this time span be? Of course that could not be answered for a past event; however, we do know the answer will be 3-1/2 years, the great tribulation time period and the reason there has never been such a time nor ever will be again.

Please do understand these things were missed by this earthly author, in past years. Yet, after being shown the proper applying of scriptures, this explanation was made possible. Things are presented in a question format to allow you to see proof of things claimed from scriptures. The Words of God should always be our guide posts.

Consider the comparison of the following verses

Mat 24:16 *then let them that are in Judaea flee unto the mountains:*
Mat 24:17 *let him that is on the housetop not go down to take out things that are in his house:*
Mat 24:18 *and let him that is in the field not return back to take his cloak.*
Mat 24:19 *But woe unto them that are with child and to them that give suck in those days!*

Mat 24:20 *And pray ye that your flight be not in the winter, neither on a sabbath:*

Compare the above with the following.

Rev 12:6 *And the woman fled into the wilderness, where she hath a place prepared of God, that there they may nourish her a thousand two hundred and threescore days.*

Rev 12:14 *And there were given to the woman the two wings of the great eagle, that she might fly into the wilderness unto her place, where she is nourished for a time, and times, and half a time, from the face of the serpent.*

It should be clear that both sets of scriptures are speaking of the same events. Thus we see the same event from different angels. We know that Mat 24:16-20 will occur when the great tribulation occurs. We can see that Rev 12:6 & 14 will occur during a time period of 3-1/2 years when Satan is kicked out of heaven.

Verse 6 says the woman will be nourished for 1260 days which of course is 3-1/2 years. Verse 14 says the woman will be nourished for time, times, and half a time. That equates to 3-1/2 years. As a future event we can see these events will happen during the time period our Lord calls great tribulation a 3-1/2 year time period. If these events are history, where in history are they found? Please stand up, step forward and point out your list in history for all to see. It is not enough just to stand and claim; you should be able to stand and back up your claims.

Rev 12:13 And when the dragon saw that he was cast down to the earth, he persecuted the woman that brought forth the man child.
Rev 12:14 And there were given to the woman the two wings of the great eagle, that she might fly into the wilderness unto her place, where she is nourished for a time, and times, and half a time, from the face of the serpent.
Rev 12:15 And the serpent cast out of his mouth after the woman water as a river, that he might cause her to be carried away by the stream.
Rev 12:16 And the earth helped the woman, and the earth opened her mouth and swallowed up the river which the dragon cast out of his mouth.

Rev 12:17 And the dragon waxed wroth with the woman, and went away to make _war_ with the rest of her seed, that keep the commandments of God, and hold the testimony of Jesus:

Chapter 12 verse 17 lists the call for war. The peaceful times of the 1st 3-1/2 years are about to come to an end. The strictly _Jewish thing_ that has occurred for the 1st 3-1/2 years is about to go worldwide. In chapter 3 verse 10, our Lord says that time will come upon the whole world to test those who live on the earth. Why will things spread out of hand unto the entire world? Verse 17 gives us that reason. Only about 40-41% of the Jewish world population lives in the Nation of Israel. That is about six million. Those pushing numbers claim; there are about fourteen million Jewish persons worldwide. The United States has a Jewish citizenry as large as or perhaps larger than the Nation of Israel. Jewish persons live over the entire world. That is the reason as stated in verse 17 that the once Jewish thing, once confined to the Nation of Israel will spread unto the entire world. This scriptural happening is yet another reason the preterits view is just off base as the time period 70 A.D. remained just a Jewish thing that never overflowed unto the entire world. The American Indians, the Alaska Eskimos and many more worldwide knew nothing about the Jewish thing of 70 A.D. Yet, when He comes at His 2nd coming all will see Him. That scripture requirement is now possible being so in just the last few years.

Many falsely believe that all the Jewish peoples have already gone home. Today, that is not the case. During the millennial reign of 1000 years on earth of our Lord Jesus Christ; He will bring _the entire_ Jewish peoples home leaving non behind, not even the dry bones. See Ezekiel chapters 37- 38.

Time frame for chapter 12 for the purpose of charting these events will occur just past the breaking of the 7 year agreement. That event will happen in the middle of the 7 year agreement just after the 1st 3-1/2 year time period and at the very beginning of the 2nd 3-1/2 year time period. There is no guess work involved as both verses 6 and 14 lists for us that precise information allowing precise time placement.

What will be seen, at that time period, is a stacking effect; multiple events taking place at the same time. We have seen that chapter 10 events will occur at the very beginning of the 2nd 3-1/2 years, that chapter 11 verses 1-6 will occur at this same time period, and now we see that chapter 12 events will also occur at the very same time period. We are about to see that the events of chapter 13 will also occur at this same time period.

The advent of so many events happening at the same time is hard for us to grasp as we do not possess mental arms long enough to wrap around and hold mentally all events at one time. Undoubtedly, that is why our Lord made the statement in Matthew 24:21-22 about this time period called the great tribulation.

Mat 24:21 *for then shall be great tribulation, such as hath not been from the beginning of the world until now, no, nor ever shall be.*
Mat 24:22 *And except those days had been shortened, no flesh would have been saved: but for the elect's sake those days shall be shortened.*

The raptured church group, that's us folks, will likely be setting on bleachers in heaven during these times of troubles taking in all the earthly events. Some may not know what is coming next as they did what some ministers say, "just wait and see," and did not bother to study the book of Revelation or they studied a man's path instead of His True Word and gained little understanding. Listen, can we hear someone asking, *"hey Jack what is going to happen next?"* It is a sincere hope that you are beginning to develop a mental program that will sever you well during our possible bleacher time. By the time we finish our way through the book of Revelation, may your mental program develop to the point of answering all questions presented both in our present life, perhaps teaching others, and on the bleachers of heaven answering questions of those who did not bother.

Chapter 13

Satan gathers his hellish team; the fall of the 7th king the rise of the 8th king the beast

Chapter 13 is a complete chapter without splitting. Chapter 13 is an earthy scene while chapter 12 is a heavenly scene, both will take place at or near the very same time.

Rev 13:1 And he stood upon the sand of the sea. And I saw a beast coming up out of the sea, having ten horns, and seven heads, and on his horns ten diadems, and upon his heads names of blasphemy.

Rev 13:2 And the beast which I saw was like unto a leopard, and his feet were as the feet of a bear, and his mouth as the mouth of a lion: and the dragon gave him his power, and his throne, and great authority.

Rev 13:3 And I saw one of his heads as though it had been smitten unto death; and his death-stroke was healed: and the whole earth wondered after the beast;

Rev 13:4 and they worshipped the dragon, because he gave his authority unto the beast; and they worshipped the beast, saying, Who is like unto the beast? And who is able to war with him?

Rev 13:5 and there was given to him a mouth speaking great things and blasphemies; and there was given to him authority to continue forty and two months.

Rev 13:6 And he opened his mouth for blasphemies against God, to blaspheme his name, and his tabernacle, even them that dwell in the heaven.

Rev 13:7 And it was given unto him to make war with the saints, and to overcome them: and there was given to him authority over every tribe and people and tongue and nation.

Rev 13:8 And all that dwell on the earth shall worship him, every one whose name hath not been written from the foundation of the world in the book of life of the Lamb that hath been slain.

Rev 13:9 If any man hath an ear, let him hear.

Rev 13:10 If any man is for captivity, into captivity he goeth: if any man shall kill with the sword, with the sword must he be killed. Here is the patience and the faith of the saints.

Rev 13:11 And I saw another beast coming up out of the earth; and he had two horns like unto a lamb, and he spake as a dragon.

Rev 13:12 And he exerciseth all the authority of the first beast in his sight. And he maketh the earth and them dwell therein to worship the first beast, whose death-stroke was healed.

Rev 13:13 And he doeth great signs, that he should even make fire to come down out of heaven upon the earth in the sight of men.

Rev 13:14 And he deceiveth them that dwell on the earth by reason of the signs which it was given him to do in the sight of the beast; saying to them that dwell on the earth, that they should make an image to the beast who hath the stroke of the sword and lived.

Rev 13:15 And it was given unto him to give breath to it, even to the image to the beast, that the image of the beast should both speak, and cause that as many as should not worship the image of the beast should be killed.

Rev 13:16 And he causeth all, the small and the great, and the rich and the poor, and the free and the bond, that there be given them a mark on their right hand, or upon their forehead;

Rev 13:17 and that no man should be able to buy or to sell, save he that hath the mark, even the name of the beast or the number of his name.

Rev 13:18 Here is wisdom. He that hath understanding, let him count the number of the beast; for it is the number of a man: and his number is Six hundred and sixty and six.

Verse 5 lists for us the length of time that the events of chapter 13 will span. A time period of 42 months which equals 3-1/2 years the same 3-1/2 years which will make up the great tribulation time period. The same 3-1/2 years that chapter 12 will occupy. Verse 7 calls for wars and that condition is about to break out over the entire world.

Chapter 11 verse 2 lists 42 months; verse 3 lists 1260 days; chapter 12 verse 6 lists 1260 days; verse 14 lists time, times, and half a time; chapter 13 verse 5 lists 42 months. We should understand that the stacking effect of multiple events is well documented. All these events plus chapter 10 will take place at the very beginning of the 2nd 3-1/2 years at the very beginning of the great tribulation. This will be the true, "*shock and awe*," announced over 1900 years ago, but, which is yet future. Will there be an aircraft carrier involved?

Likely no announcement will be made from an aircraft carrier.

The 7th king, the antichrist will make a 7 year covenant agreement with the Nation of Israel. He will break that agreement after just 3-1/2 years. Chapter 17 tells that the 7th king will rule for a little while. That little while is 3-1/2 years, the 1st 3-1/2 years that the agreement holds. He will then give himself to the spirit of Satan, he will be indwelled by Satan, and will become the 8th king, the beast. We see in verse 4 that the beast derives his power from Satan. We see Satan will rule for a time period of 3-1/2 years. That 3-1/2 years will be the 2nd 3-1/2 years of the 7 year time period. We see Paul telling the same thing in 2 Thes 2:3-9.

2Th 2:3 *let no man beguile you in any wise: for it will not be, except the falling away come first, and the man of sin be* revealed, *the son of perdition,*

2Th 2:4 *he that opposeth and exalteth himself against all that is called God or that is worshipped; so that he sitteth in the temple of God, setting himself forth as God.*

2Th 2:5 *Remember ye not, that, when I was yet with you, I told you these things?*

2Th 2:6 *And now ye know that which* restraineth, *to the end that he may be* revealed *in his own season.*

2Th 2:7 *For the mystery of lawlessness doth already work: only there is one that* restraineth *now, until he be taken out of the way.*

2Th 2:8 *And then shall be* revealed *the lawless one, whom the Lord Jesus shall slay with the breath of his mouth, and bring to nought by the manifestation of his coming;*

2Th 2:9 *even he, whose coming is according to the working of Satan with all power and signs and lying wonders,*

Paul calls this person the man of sin, the son of perdition. Other Bible versions call him the son of lawlessness, the son of destruction. Paul says three times that this person will be revealed. The preterits view which attributes the events of Daniel and Revelation to a time period around 70 A.D. the time of the destruction of the 2nd temple; those holding this view should be able to stand up and to tell the whole world the name of this person as 70 A.D. is history of almost 2000 years. Of course they cannot. The name of this person is not given as it is not known as the events of Daniel and Revelation are not history they are future events which will come to past and then the name of this person will be known as Paul has listed. Paul also lists for us that the *restrainer* will be taken out of the way. This is a reference to the Holy Spirit who is now at work in this world. At the beginning of the great tribulation, the 2nd 3-1/3 year time period, the Holy Spirit, will for a time, be taken from this world giving Satan and his hellish trinity unhindered access to work his self thought wonders. This un-hindering is a testament to the power of our Lord Jesus Christ, meaning Satan will not be able to stand before our Lord.

At this time the 3rd temple is taken over, sacrifices will be stopped; the abomination of desolation will be setup in the holy place of the temple.

Mat 24:15 *When therefore ye see the abomination of desolation, which was spoken of through Daniel the prophet, standing in the holy place (let him that readeth understand),*

We should be at least grasping the handle of understanding by this point in this revealing. Yes, there are a lot of events yet to come, but, a lot of territory has been covered and a feel for the things of Revelation should be taking shape. You should be realizing, that understanding can be made of Revelation and that you should not be just waiting to see what will happen. You have in your hands the further revealing giving you understanding.

Chapter 13 is giving us detailed information about the gathering of Satan's command structure and his coming activities.

Satan is not an originator, he is an imitator. As such he follows the pattern of our heavenly trinity, God the Father, our Lord Jesus Christ and the Holy Spirit. Satan's trinity includes himself in the roll of Almighty, the beast in the roll of Jesus Christ, and the false prophet in the roll of the Holy Spirit.

By now there will have been war in heaven and Satan with his fallen angels will be thrown out of heaven as listed in chapter 12 verses 7, 8, and 9.. He has gathered his hellish trinity, and is going to pursue the Jewish peoples and the saints of God over the entire world, as he knows he has but a short time. The Jewish thing is about to blossom into full world wars. Soon all will find there is no place on earth to hide as will be seen when the 6th seal is broken.

With both chapters 12 and 13 calling for wars and the 2nd seal judgment taking peace from the world, it is time to honor the call for wars as now the time known as great tribulation is in season. Now the breaking of the 2nd seal will not cause problems between scripture verses. There will not be one scripture stepping on the toes of another scripture, all will be in harmony.

Your chart should have chapter 6 verses 1 and 2 placed at the very beginning of the 1st 3-1/2 year time period. Chapter 7 verses 1-8 should be charted at the very end of the 1st 3-1/2 years. Then will occur a event stacking time period as many events will happen at the very same time. Chapter 10, chapter 11 verses 1-8, chapters 12 and 13 events will all take place at the very beginning of the 2nd 3-1/2 year time period. This will be the *true shock and awe*. This of course is the start of the great tribulation time period which will last 3-1/2 years culminating with the 2nd coming of our Lord Jesus Christ.

Our next move could be to chapter 14 from this point, however, chapter 14 does not belong in its numeric listing, with explanations following.

A brief explanation concerning the placement of chapter 14 will be discussed here. This subject in and of itself causes confusion that man just has not been able to overcome. What follows is not an opinion. The placement of chapter 14 has always been directed by our Lord Jesus Christ. He placed in the words of Revelation over 1900 years ago, directions showing man just where chapter 14 belongs. Man has seen but has not followed directions.

Have you ever purchased a knock down piece of furniture then followed the included directions to put the furniture together? Our Lord did a similar thing in Revelation concerning chapter 14. When we reach the time period that chapter 14 belongs in, complete directions will be given. But for now, we will set aside chapter 14 and we will proceed with the next events in the time sequence.

Chapter 6 verses 3-8

The 2nd, 3rd, and 4th seal judgments
Red horse rider the 2nd seal takes peace from the world
Black horse rider the 3rd seal brings famines
Pale horse rider the 4th seal brings plagues to the entire world.

Peace taken, famines, and plagues, 1.8 billion die

The holding vessel chapter 6 is revisited to retrieve additional contents. Like a 2nd visit to a cookie jar more of the contents are taken yet some still remain.

Rev 6:3 And when he opened the second seal, I heard the second living creature saying, Come.

Rev 6:4 And another horse came forth, a red horse: and to him that sat thereon it was given to take peace from the earth, and that they should slay one another: and there was given unto him a great sword.

Rev 6:5 And when he opened the third seal, I heard the third living creature saying, Come. And I saw, and behold, a black horse; and he that sat thereon had a balance in his hand.

Rev 6:6 And I heard as it were a voice in the midst of the four living creatures saying, A measure of wheat for a shilling, and three measures of barley for a shilling; and the oil and the wine hurt thou not.

Rev 6:7 And when he opened the fourth seal, I heard the voice of the fourth living creature saying, Come.

Rev 6:8 And I saw, and behold, a pale horse: and he that sat upon him, his name was Death; and Hades followed with him. And there was given unto them authority over the fourth part of the earth, to kill with sword, and with famine, and with death, and by the wild beasts of the earth.

At this time the 2nd seal judgment is appropriate to be broken as chapters 12 and 13 both call for wars. No scriptures are found to be out of harmony by breaking this seal at this time. No scriptures are stepping on the toes of other scriptures. The agreement will have been broken; the time period is in the great tribulation. Both chapters 12 and 13 have called for wars and the 2nd seal takes peace from the world. What results when peace is taken? All is in harmony and all is making perfect sense. The 3rd and 4th seal judgments are close cousins to wars, as famines and plagues will follow hostilities and many times kill more persons than the actual battles of wars.

Thus the 2nd, 3rd, and 4th seals will all be broken within a very short time period. Likely no more than one year will past before the carnage of these three seal judgments is fully felt all over the entire world. One fourth of the world's population will lay dead. By numbers listed for the year 2012, 7.2 <u>billion</u> people occupy this earth. One fourth of that number equals 1.8 <u>billion</u> people who will lose their lives.

That number is so large how do we understand the gravity of that amount of people being killed within a short time. We learn by comparison. World War II lasted for many about 7 years. During that time period around 60 <u>million</u> persons lost their lives. That number represents about 0.03 percent of the 1.8 <u>billion</u> that will lose their lives during the opening volley of the great tribulation.

Certainly, our Lord's words ring out, that the great tribulation will be unlike any time past nor ever will be again, and allows us to know, these times to date, have not occurred.

Yet the 1.8 <u>billion</u> is only the 1st round. That amount again will be killed in a later volley of events, when a 200 <u>million</u> man army crosses the Euphrates River. Over one half of the earth's population will lose their lives during the great tribulation. The Lord's words; don't let anyone deceive you; these things have not yet taken place, yet today so many are confused and deceived and told just wait and see. With many more making claims that the things of Revelation will never come to past. Many churches will not teach Revelation, in its true form, because of misunderstandings and they do not want to frighten their parishioners. But, does man really have those rights? Can we follow Him yet be selective as to what we follow? Seems many think they can yet the Lord says all have gone their own way.

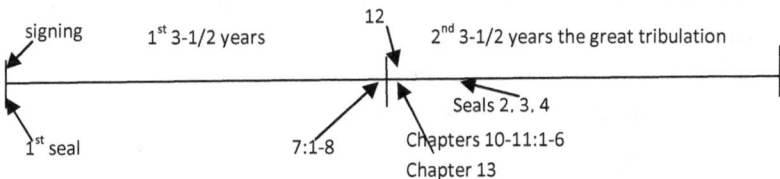

signing   1st 3-1/2 years   12   2nd 3-1/2 years the great tribulation

1st seal   7:1-8   Seals 2, 3, 4

Chapters 10-11:1-6

Chapter 13

Chapter 6 verses 9-11

5th seal judgment
1st martyred group in heaven, this is a rapture but not the church as the church group has been raptured into the present heaven and are listed in the present heaven in chapter 5 verses 9 and 10.

Rev 6:9 And when he opened the fifth seal, I saw underneath the altar the souls of them that had been slain for the word of God, and for the testimony which they held:
Rev 6:10 and they cried with a great voice, saying, How long, O Master, the holy and true, dost thou not judge and avenge our blood on them that dwell on the earth?
Rev 6:11 And there was given them to each one a white robe; and it was said unto them, that they should rest yet for a little time, until their fellow-servants also and their brethren, who should be killed even as they were, should have fulfilled their course.

When the 5th seal judgment is broken, a heavenly scene reveals a number of saved, from those killed from the 1st 1.8 <u>billion</u> involving the 2nd, 3rd, and 4th seal judgments. We have no way of knowing the size of this group. We only know that this group is the saved from that huge group that will be killed. What we can extract from the information given is that this group is made up of new Christians saved during the time period after the rapture of the church group, which will have happened over 4-1/2 years earlier. If this group had been saved at the time of the rapture of the church, this group would have been rapture with the church group and would now be in heaven. Some claim this group is the church group raptured as med-tribulation rapture. However, this time frame is not at the med point of the 7 years, this time frame will occur at least one year after the med point. No rapture takes place at or near the med point of the 7 years. The mid-tribulation rapture is another error due to following a strict chronological view of Revelation.

This group is likely to be the work of the 144,000 who perhaps will be witnessing unto the entire world. Part of this group could be the work of the two witnesses witnessing to the Nation of Israel. This could mean that all or most of this group will be saved during the great tribulation, not prior to the great tribulation. This group could be new Christians saved after the protection of both the 144,000 and the two witnesses. This group will defy the order of the false prophet seen in chapter 13 to take the mark of the beast. Worship of Satan or the beast in any way is the unforgivable sin. We are not told the ethnic makeup of this group. This group is likely from all over the entire world from many different countries and peoples. The size of this group is anyone's guess as no figures are shared. This group could range in size from a few people to <u>millions or to multi millions</u>.

Time frame for charting. This group likely will appear in heaven, a rapture, within the first year after hostilities break out worldwide. That would be about 30 months before the 2nd coming or 4-1/2 years past the signing of the 7 year agreement. They are given white robes and told to wait a little while as their numbers will grow as more martyred will be added. We will see a later group added that die in the same way as will this group.

73

Chapter 6 verses 12-17

6th seal judgment an earthly scene
chapter 6-holding vessel, a cookie jar is now emptied

Rev 6:12 And I saw when he opened the sixth seal, and there was a great earthquake; and the sun became black as sackcloth of hair, and the whole moon became as blood;
Rev 6:13 and the stars of the heaven fell unto the earth, as a fig tree casteth her unripe figs when she is shaken of a great wind.
Rev 6:14 And the heaven was removed as a scroll when it is rolled up; and every mountain and island were moved out of their places.
Rev 6:15 And the kings of the earth, and the princes, and the chief captains, and the rich, and the strong, and every bondman and freeman, hid themselves in the caves and in the rocks of the mountains;
Rev 6:16 and they say to the mountains and to the rocks, Fall on us, and hide us from the face of him that sitteth on the throne, and from the wrath of the Lamb:
Rev 6:17 for the great day of their wrath is come; and who is able to stand?

The 6th seal judgment is an earthly scene of continuing hellish like conditions. Again this will be a time like never before nor ever will be again. By these descriptions we know that these conditions are yet in our future as no such actions have ever been known on earth. Some claim and I have been asked if the holocaust of WWII were these conditions and that the things of Revelation have already happened. Yet as bad as the conditions were of WWII, those conditions will seem pale to the conditions of the great tribulation. Our minds do not want to except that these conditions will one day be upon this earth. We do not want to except that the things of Revelation will come upon mankind. Our minds tell us that these things just will not happen. Seemingly, one of the reasons the book of Revelation is shied away from by many churches is that some in charge of churches do not want to upset the congregation. Yet God's Words will be completed to the 777 standards of God, and are not controlled nor depend on the 666 standards of man. Some say, "just wait and see,"

The great tribulation is going to be unlike the two so called world wars in that the great tribulation will be a true world war with no places on earth to hide. A number of countries did not experience actual battles during both WWI and WWII. Places existed where vacations could be taken far away from the possibility of war. That will not be the case during the great tribulation, there will be no place on earth to hide. This is seen in chapter 6 verses 12-17 as then all on the earth will fully realize the judgment of this world has come and will fully realize who has brought the judgment. That realization sadly will not stop many from taking the mark of the beast.

Chapter 8 verses 1-6

7th seal judgment
a heavenly scene, one cookie jar emptied another visited

Rev 8:1 And when he opened the seventh seal, there followed a silence in heaven about the space of half an hour.

Hope all caught and seen the stilts being knocked out from under the claim of a strict chronological reading of the book of Revelation. The seal judgments are separated being listed in both chapter 6 and chapter 8. Skipping over chapter 7 which does not house any seal judgments. A strict reading means that all of chapter 6, all of chapter 7, and part of chapter 8 would have to take place in the 1st 3-1/2 years which of course would cause problems with scriptures harmonizing.

It is likely that the 6th and 7th seal judgments will occur at or near the same time. It is likely that the earthquake seen in both seal judgments is the same earthquake. The 6th seal judgment is an earthly scene while the 7th seal judgment is a heavenly scene. Now the 7 sealed scrolls our Lord as a lamb took from the hand of the Heavenly Father, in chapter 5, has had all 7 seals broken. This is the reason the little open book of chapter 10 could not be the 7 sealed scroll our Lord has in hand, as that scroll was still on duty, still in service, while the 7 year covenant agreement had been broken.

Time frame for charting; this becomes a guessing game to an extent. Chapter 10, part of chapter 11, all of chapters 12 and 13 can be precisely positioned upon a time line representing the 7 year time period which will make up the hour of testing. Of course we cannot attach calendar dates to these 7 years. Therefore, a time frame chart will not be relational to a calendar, but, can represent spacing within the known 7 year hour of testing.

Most events will take place in the 2nd half of this 7 year period. That time period is called by our Lord the great tribulation. Some confuse this time period and falsely refer to this time period as the entire 7 years. The full 7 year time period is called by many the tribulation time period, while the last 3-1/2 years will be the great tribulation time period. Mat 24:15 clearly will be an event which will take place in the middle of Daniel's prophecy of the 70th week. Mat 24:21 which lists for us the information about the great tribulation is a continuance of the subject matter of Mat 24:15, which clearly will happen in the middle of the 7 year time period. Therefore, it is known the great tribulation is not the entire 7 year time period and is the 2nd half of the 7 year time period the last 3-1/2 years of that 7 years. Sounds like harping, perhaps, yet this is a point of much confusion while understanding is our goal. Like climbing a stairs, we must use all steps; this is one of the steps which must be realized.

Time frame for charting the 6th and 7th seal judgments; these judgments will occur before the 21 month mark of the last 3-1/2 year time period. This means the cookie jar, chapter 6 will be emptied of all contents about 21 months into the (2) 3-1/2 years, about 21 months into the great tribulation, or before the 2nd coming. The cookie jar of chapter 8 will be emptied of the 7th seal judgment, but, will still contain trumpet judgments.

In the last 42 months of the 7 year time period, there are no less than 50 events that will take place. As it is said, it is a full plate, or slate. Many of these events do not have given ways of precisely placing them on a time chart. However, do to the packed house of events and the fact that some of the events do have known placements; the remaining events without known placements can be assigned a reasonable time frame placement. Please know there would be little wiggle room for events assigned a reasonable time frame. Placing 50 events into 42 months means, by time limitation, the assigned time frames would have to be close to the actual time frames.

We know for sure what is given for sure; we know for sure that all scripture will take place as given.

Mat 5:18 *For verily I say unto you, Till heaven and earth pass away, one jot or one tittle shall in no wise pass away from the law, till all things be accomplished.*

A point has come in this presentation of transitioning from the seal judgments to the trumpet judgments. The journey through Revelation has lead to chapter 8 listing the 7th seal judgment which terminates the seal judgments. Now will come the 7 trumpet judgments which clearly follow the 7 seal judgments. We can see that the 7 trumpet judgments are ready to be administered.

Note the resemblance between chapter 5 verse 8 and chapter 8 verses 3-5.

Rev 5:8 *When He took the scroll, the four living creatures and the 24 elders fell down before the Lamb. Each one had a harp and gold bowls filled with incense, which are the prayers of the saints.*

Rev 8:2 Then I saw the seven angels who stand in the presence of God; seven trumpets were given to them.
Rev 8:3 Another angel, with a gold incense burner, came and stood at the altar. He was given a large amount of incense to offer with the prayers of all the saints on the gold altar in front of the throne.
Rev 8:4 The smoke of the incense, with the prayers of the saints, went up in the presence of God from the angel's hand.
Rev 8:5 The angel took the incense burner, filled it with fire from the altar, and hurled it to the earth; there were rumblings of thunder, flashes of lightning, and an earthquake.

The 7 trumpet judgments are ready to be administered; however, there is a problem. It is known that the 6th trumpet and the 6th bowl judgments will be administered at or very near the same time. It can be seen that the 7th trumpet and the 7th bowl judgments will be administered at or near the same time. Yet by following the remainder of chapter 8, then chapter 9, then jumping to chapter 11 verse 15 for the 7th trumpet, does not allow the rendering of the 6th and 7th trumpet and bowl judgments to be administered at or near the same time. It is obvious another path is taken for administering the trumpet and bowl judgments.

Chapter 15 lists the prefatory information about the 7 bowl judgments. Therefore, all of chapter 15 follows chapter 8 verse 5, just before the 1st trumpet judgment is sounded. Yes, this seems a little nutty, but, evidence will show that the trumpet and bowl judgments will be administered at or near the same times.

Chapter 15, 7 bowl judgments
complete chapter no splitting of verses the angels are ready to pour

Rev 15:1 Then I saw another great and awe-inspiring sign in heaven: seven angels with the seven last plagues, for with them, God's wrath will be completed.

Rev 15:2 I also saw something like a sea of glass mixed with fire, and those who had won the victory over the beast, his image, and the number of his name, were standing on the sea of glass with harps from God.

Rev 15:3 They sang the song of God's servant Moses and the song of the Lamb: Great and awe-inspiring are Your works, Lord God, the Almighty; righteous and true are Your ways, King of the Nations.

Rev 15:4 Lord, who will not fear and glorify Your name? Because You alone are holy, for all the nations will come and worship before You because Your righteous acts have been revealed.

Rev 15:5 After this I looked, and the heavenly sanctuary--the tabernacle of testimony--was opened.

Rev 15:6 Out of the sanctuary came the seven angels with the seven plagues, dressed in clean, bright linen, with gold sashes wrapped around their chests.

Rev 15:7 One of the four living creatures gave the seven angels seven gold bowls filled with the wrath of God who lives forever and ever.

Rev 15:8 Then the sanctuary was filled with smoke from God's glory and from His power, and no one could enter the sanctuary until the seven plagues of the seven angels were completed.

Searching for answers it is noticed that chapter 17 follows the Euphrates River crossing which is the 6th trumpet judgment. It is noted that chapter 17 verse 1 says, "And there came one of the seven angels *that had* the seven bowls, and spake with me, saying, Come hither, I will show thee the judgment of the great harlot that sitteth upon many waters;

Now we see that bowl judgments will be poured out before the 7th trumpet judgment has sounded, as chapter 17 will occur before the 2nd coming. The 7th trumpet will sound when the mysteries of God's plan is complete. That is the 2nd coming. By scriptures we now know that bowl judgments will be poured out before all the trumpet judgments have been completed. When we look at the 7th bowl judgment found in chapter 16 verse 17 we find the claim made by the 7th trumpet judgment is also a claim made be the 7th bowl judgment. Both judgments are claiming to be the finishing point of the great tribulation. How could that be other than both judgments will occur at the very same time?

If the 7th trumpet and 7th bowl judgments will occur at the same time, perhaps that holds true for other trumpet and bowl judgments. Actually, the 7th bowl judgment will be administered slightly before the 7th trumpet judgment. How is that known? That is known because of chapter 15 verse 8. It is said that no one can enter the temple until all seven plagues or bowl judgments are poured out. Yet, chapter 11 verse 19 says there was open the temple. Thus in order for the sequence to happen, the 7th bowl judgment must be administered before the 7th trumpet judgment.

Looking at the 6th trumpet and 6th bowl judgments, it is found that both deal with the Euphrates River crossing. However, the 6th bowl judgments dries up the river allowing an easier crossing which takes place as listed in the 6th trumpet judgment. Therefore, by the Word of God, the 6th bowl judgment will be administered before the 6th trumpet judgment. Things must measure to the 777 level of God. It is looking like the claim the bowl judgments follow the trumpet judgments is a path from the 666 level of man and is not the path of God.

From the evidence found in scriptures both the trumpet and bowl judgments will be administered at or near the very same time from the 1st to the last of these judgments.

Rev 8:6 And the seven angels that had the seven trumpets prepared themselves to sound.

It was stated earlier that a spirit of our Lord revealed the path of Revelation, to this earthly author and that was what happened. It was also said that the proof is in the pudding, (in the scriptures of the book of Revelation). Before the Spirit revealing this person had no more knowledge of event placement of Revelation than anyone else. This person read over the scripture proofs without realizing their presents. In order to reveal to you the proofs, scriptures are pointed out containing those proofs. Although presented as if we are chasing down leads as we go, you must see the things that have always been there, yet, missed by man, that is why the progress is listed in this manner. Please do understand that nothing new is being given. What is being revealed has always been part of the scriptures making up the book of Revelation. These things are not an itching ear teaching of new information.

We need to realize that just before the 2nd coming is; at the very end of the (2) 3-1/2 years, at the very end of the great tribulation, and time will run out for the administration of judgments. Both the trumpet and bowl judgments are claiming the job of ending the great tribulation, but, that could only happen if both judgments are administered at or near the same time. Our continuance will be based upon the assumption that both the trumpet and bowl judgments will occur at or near the same times. Perhaps that continuance will reveal a clear path. Following is presented the trumpet and bowl judgments being administered in tandem.

Chapter 8 verse 7 the 1st trumpet is sounded

Chapter 16 verses 1 and 2 the 1st bowl judgment is poured out. *No particular connection is seen between the 1st trumpet and bowl judgments.*

Rev 8:7 And the first sounded, and there followed hail and fire, mingled with blood, and they were cast upon the earth: and the third part of the earth was burnt up, and the third part of the trees was burnt up, and all green grass was burnt up.

Rev 16:1 And I heard a great voice out of the temple, saying to the seven angels, Go ye, and pour out the seven bowls of the wrath of God into the earth.

Rev 16:2 And the first went, and poured out his bowl into the earth; and it became a noisome and grievous sore upon the men that had the mark of the beast, and that worshipped his image.

Chapter 8 verses 8 and 9 the 2nd trumpet is sounded
Chapter 16 verse 3 the 2nd bowl judgment is poured out
A great similarity between the 2nd trumpet and bowl judgments is seen

Rev 8:8 And the second angel sounded, and as it were a great mountain burning with fire was cast into the sea: and the third part of the sea became blood;

Rev 8:9 and there died the third part of the creatures which were in the sea, even they that had life; and the third part of the ships was destroyed.

Rev 16:3 And the second poured out his bowl into the sea; and it became blood as of a dead man; and every living soul died, even the things that were in the sea.

Chapter 8 verses 10-11 the 3rd trumpet judgment is sounded
Chapter 16 verses 4-7 the 3rd bowl judgment is poured out
A great similarity between the 3nd trumpet and bowl judgments is seen

Rev 8:10 And the third angel sounded, and there fell from heaven a great star, burning as a torch, and it fell upon the third part of the rivers, and upon the fountains of the waters;

Rev 8:11 and the name of the star is called Wormwood: and the third part of the waters became wormwood; and many men died of the waters, because they were made bitter.

Rev 16:4 And the third poured out his bowl into the rivers and the fountains of the waters; and it became blood.

Rev 16:5 And I heard the angel of the waters saying, Righteous art thou, who art and who wast, thou Holy One, because thou didst thus judge:

Rev 16:6 for they poured out the blood of the saints and the prophets, and blood hast thou given them to drink: they are worthy.

Rev 16:7 And I heard the altar saying, Yea, O Lord God, the Almighty, true and righteous are thy judgments.

Chapter 8 verses 12-13 the 4th trumpet judgment is sounded
Chapter 16 verses 8-9 the 4th bowl judgment is poured out
A great similarity between the 4nd trumpet and bowl judgments is seen

Rev 8:12 And the fourth angel sounded, and the third part of the sun was smitten, and the third part of the moon, and the third part of the stars; that the third part of them should be darkened, and the day should not shine for the third part of it, and the night in like manner.

Rev 8:13 And I saw, and I heard an eagle, flying in mid heaven, saying with a great voice, Woe, woe, woe, for them that dwell on the earth, by reason of the other voices of the trumpet of the three angels, who are yet to sound.

Rev 16:8 And the fourth poured out his bowl upon the sun; and it was given unto it to scorch men with fire.

Rev 16:9 And men were scorched with great heat: and they blasphemed the name of God who hath the power over these plagues; and they repented not to give him glory.

Chapter 9 verses 1-12 the 5th trumpet judgment is sounded
Chapter 16 verses 10-11 the 5th bowl judgment is poured out.

There is a similarity between the 5th trumpet and bowl judgments in that the 5th trumpet judgment is upon those who have not the mark of God on their foreheads. While the 5th bowl judgment will be poured out upon the beast himself. In other words the 5th trumpet is administered on those following Satan and beast while the 5th bowl judgments is poured out on the throne of the beast. One goes after the body, the other goes after the head.

For those of us who have been stung by a scorpion chapter 9 verses 1-12 brings back a time to be forgotten. Thinking back on that experience and remembering the intense pain which lasted for days, the thought of that pain lasting for months implants sheer terror. Living then in scorpion country, I was told before the sting; oh it's like a bee sting if it happens. I have been stung, over the years, by a number of different bees and no bee sting that I had received came close to the pain level or rendered the effects of a scorpion sting. Along with the intense pain level were the effects on the eyes, on my voice, the effect of water tasting so salty you did not want the water in your mouth and would spit it out. The sting occurred when the outside temperature was above 100 degree.

The 5th trumpet and bowl judgment perhaps is the fulfillment of Dan 9:27 in part which says; and even unto the full end, and that determined, shall wrath be poured out upon the desolate. Of course the desolate will be Satan and his beast. Please read the 5th bowl judgment.

Rev 9:1 And the fifth angel sounded, and I saw a star from heaven fallen unto the earth: and there was given to him the key of the pit of the abyss.
Rev 9:2 And he opened the pit of the abyss; and there went up a smoke out of the pit, as the smoke of a great furnace; and the sun and the air were darkened by reason of the smoke of the pit.
Rev 9:3 And out of the smoke came forth locusts upon the earth; and power was given them, as the scorpions of the earth have power.
Rev 9:4 And it was said unto them that they should not hurt the grass of the earth, neither any green thing, neither any tree, but only such men as have not the seal of God on their foreheads.
Rev 9:5 And it was given them that they should not kill them, but that they should be tormented five months: and their torment was as the torment of a scorpion, when it striketh a man.
Rev 9:6 And in those days men shall seek death, and shall in no wise find it; and they shall desire to die, and death fleeth from them.
Rev 9:7 And the shapes of the locusts were like unto horses prepared for war; and upon their heads as it were crowns like unto gold, and their faces were as men's faces.
Rev 9:8 And they had hair as the hair of women, and their teeth were as the teeth of lions.
Rev 9:9 And they had breastplates, as it were breastplates of iron; and the

sound of their wings was as the sound of chariots, of many horses rushing to war.

Rev 9:10 And they have tails like unto scorpions, and stings; and in their tails is their power to hurt men five months.

Rev 9:11 They have over them as king the angel of the abyss: his name in Hebrew is Abaddon, and in the Greek tongue he hath the name Apollyon.

Rev 9:12 The first Woe is past: behold, there come yet two Woes hereafter.

Rev 16:10 And the fifth poured out his bowl upon the throne of the beast; and his kingdom was darkened; and they gnawed their tongues for pain,

Rev 16:11 and they blasphemed the God of heaven because of their pains and their sores; and they repented not of their works.

For charting purposes the 5ᵗʰ trumpet and bowl judgments are assigned a time frame of 18 months before the 2ⁿᵈ coming. The 5ᵗʰ seal judgment will last for five months as listed in verses 5

Chapter 9 verses 13-21 the 6ᵗʰ trumpet judgment is sounded
Chapter 16 verses 12-16 the 6ᵗʰ bowl judgment is poured out

A great similarity between the 6ⁿᵈ trumpet and bowl judgments the crossing of the Euphrates River

The 6ᵗʰ bowl and 6ᵗʰ trumpet judgments will either be administered at or near the same time or there would have to be two river crossings. Actually, the 6ᵗʰ bowl judgment will be administered ahead of the 6ᵗʰ trumpet judgment as the river bed is dried up to allow an easier crossing. The likelihood of there being two river crossings can be ruled out for lack of supporting scripture information and the lack of time to administer. As was noted before, there is already a full plate of events and the addition of a 2ⁿᵈ river crossing would totally overflow the existing time.

This would mean that _yes_ indeed the trumpet and bowl judgments will be administered at or near the same times.

Rev 9:13 And the sixth angel sounded, and I heard a voice from the horns of the golden altar which is before God,

Rev 9:14 one saying to the sixth angel that had one trumpet, Loose the four angels that are bound at the great river Euphrates.

Rev 9:15 And the four angels were loosed, that had been prepared for the hour and day and month and year, that they should kill the third part of men.

Rev 9:16 And the number of the armies of the horsemen was twice ten thousand times ten thousand: I heard the number of them.

Rev 9:17 And thus I saw the horses in the vision, and them that sat on them, having breastplates as of fire and of hyacinth and of brimstone: and the heads of lions; and out of their mouths proceedeth fire and smoke and brimstone.

Rev 9:18 By these three plagues was the third part of men killed, by the fire and the smoke and the brimstone, which proceeded out of their mouths.

Rev 9:19 For the power of the horses is in their mouth, and in their tails: for their tails are like unto serpents, and have heads; and with them they hurt.

Rev 9:20 And the rest of mankind, who were not killed with these plagues, repented not of the works of their hands, that they should not worship demons, and the idols of gold, and of silver, and of brass, and of stone, and of wood; which can neither see, nor hear, nor walk:

Rev 9:21 and they repented not of their murders, nor of their sorceries, nor of their fornication, nor of their thefts.

Rev 16:12 And the sixth poured out his bowl upon the great river, the river Euphrates; and the water thereof was dried up, that the way might by made ready for the kings that come from the sunrising.

Rev 16:13 And I saw coming out of the mouth of the dragon, and out of the mouth of the beast, and out of the mouth of the false prophet, three unclean spirits, as it were frogs:

Rev 16:14 for they are spirits of demons, working signs; which go forth unto the kings of the whole world, to gather them together unto the war of the great day of God, the Almighty.

Rev 16:15 (Behold, I come as a thief. Blessed is he that watcheth, and keepeth his garments, lest he walk naked, and they see his shame.)

Rev 16:16 And they gathered them together into the place which is called in Hebrew Har-Magedon.

Chapter 9 verse 15 conveys the grim event of another huge group of mankind being killed due to the actions of the 200 million man army crossing the Euphrates River. These actions should not be confused with the battle of Armageddon. The river crossing will occur about 13

months before the battle of Armageddon. Previously, one fourth of the world population was listed as being killed due to the 2nd, 3rd, and 4th seal judgments. That amount will be around 1.8 billion, that was the 1st volley. Now that same size group will be killed by a 200 million man army, which is the 2nd volley. The two volleys will occur about 18 months apart. The earth's population started out at 7.2 billion, by 2012 estimate. 1.8 billion being removed, in 1st volley, leaves 5.4 billion. Now another 1.8 billion, the 2nd volley, a third of 5.4 billion will be killed reducing earth's population to around 3.6 billion. One half of the world's population is killed in less than 3-1/2 years called the great tribulation. Yet the death toll is not yet complete. We are later told about 7,000 killed, we do not know the number killed at Armageddon, which is yet to come and is likely a very large number. That number seemingly will be above the 200 million that crosses the river, as all the unsaved will be killed. The head count that lives through the great tribulation and enters into the millennial reign certainly is not known. Yet, we do have our Lord's words saying in Mat 24:22 and except those days had been shortened, no flesh would have been saved; but for the elect's sake those days shall be shortened.

The 7th trumpet and 7th bowl judgments cannot be presented at this time as many events will take place between the 6th trumpet and bowl judgments and the 7th trumpet and bowl judgments.

Time frame for charting of the 1st six trumpet and bowl judgments will range from about 21 months before the 2nd coming to within 13 months before the 2nd coming. As can be seen these 8 months will be unlike any period of time of the past. These are guess-a-mint time assignments, yet, should be in close proximity of real times.

Many may oppose that the trumpet and bowl judgments will be administered at or near the same times. Question; is that opposition based upon scriptures or just man's opposition? When an examination is made of the 7th trumpet and 7th bowl judgments those judgments also will take place at or near the same time, both will take place at the time of the 2nd coming. The contention that the bowl judgments follow the trumpet judgments does not have support in the pages of Revelation and is another rendering as God's Word with origins from man. We can see that the last 42 months, which is the last 3-1/2 years has a crowed agenda with the trumpet and bowl judgment running in consort. Subtracting the time for the bowl judgments to stand alone in time would create a near imposable situation. We should not allow our minds to wonder about this subject, we should rely on God's Word. Hopefully, you can see that Revelation is a lot more revealing than most of us realize. All these things have always been in the writing of Revelation, but, when we read we tend to read the high spots and forget to absorb the finer points.

Again the saying of Rev 10:7 but in the days of the voice of the seventh angel, when he is about to sound, <u>then is finished the mystery of God</u>, Again the saying of Rev 16:17 <u>saying, It is done:</u> This is supporting scripture evidence that the 7th trumpet and the 7th bowl judgments will occur at the same time.

Supporting evidence that the book of Revelation is out of chorological order is found throughout its pages. The 2nd coming is listed in <u>*chapter 19 verses 11-16*</u>. The 7th trumpet which will sound just before the 2nd coming is found in <u>*chapter 11 verses 15-19*</u>. The 7th bowl judgment which will occur just before the 2nd coming at the same time the 7th trumpet is sounded is found in <u>*chapter 16 verses 17-21*</u>.

Series of events:

16:17-21 7th bowl
11:15-19 7th trumpets
19:11-16 2nd coming

These placements constitute proof of nonaligned chronology, but, there is more, much more. No, nothing has been changed after John pinned what he was given from the Master Author Jesus Christ. Recognizing these factors of Revelation will render understanding, denying their existence fosters confusion. Denying requires scripture support. No claim of man concerning the Word of God, should be based upon man's thoughts without the solid backup of scriptures. The teachings of man, does not override the Words of God.

Rev 11:15 And the seventh angel sounded; and there followed great voices in heaven, and they said, The kingdom of the world is become the kingdom of our Lord, and of his Christ: and he shall reign for ever and ever.

Rev 11:16 And the four and twenty elders, who sit before God on their thrones, fell upon their faces and worshipped God,

Rev 11:17 saying, We give thee thanks, O Lord God, the Almighty, who art and who wast; because thou hast taken thy great power, and didst reign.

Rev 11:18 And the nations were wroth, and thy wrath came, and the time of the dead to be judged, and the time to give their reward to thy servants the prophets, and to the saints, and to them that fear thy name, the small and the great; and to destroy them that destroy the earth.

Rev 11:19 And there was opened the temple of God that is in heaven; and there was seen in his temple the ark of his covenant; and there followed lightnings, and voices, and thunders, and an earthquake, and great hail.

Rev 16:17 And the seventh poured out his bowl upon the air; and there came forth a great voice out of the temple, from the throne, saying, It is done:

Rev 16:18 and there were lightnings, and voices, and thunders; and there was a great earthquake, such as was not since there were men upon the earth, so great an earthquake, so mighty.

Rev 16:19 And the great city was divided into three parts, and the cities of the nations fell: and Babylon the great was remembered in the sight of God, to give unto her the cup of the wine of the fierceness of his wrath.

Rev 16:20 And every island fled away, and the mountains were not found.

Rev 16:21 And great hail, every stone about the weight of a talent, cometh down out of heaven upon men: and men blasphemed God because of the plague of the hail; for the plague thereof is exceeding great.

Chapter 17

Is a complete chapter without verse splitting, the harlot church, meaning of the 7 heads and 10 horns

Rev 17:1 And there came one of the seven angels ***that had*** the seven bowls, and spake with me, saying, Come hither, I will show thee the judgment of the great harlot that sitteth upon many waters;

Rev 17:2 with whom the kings of the earth committed fornication, and they that dwell in the earth were made drunken with the wine of her fornication.

Rev 17:3 And he carried me away in the Spirit into a wilderness: and I saw a woman sitting upon a scarlet-colored beast, full of names of blasphemy, having seven heads and ten horns.

Rev 17:4 And the woman was arrayed in purple and scarlet, and decked with gold and precious stone and pearls, having in her hand a golden cup full of abominations, even the unclean things of her fornication,

Rev 17:5 and upon her forehead a name written, MYSTERY, BABYLON THE GREAT, THE MOTHER OF THE HARLOTS AND OF THE ABOMINATIONS OF THE EARTH.

Rev 17:6 And I saw the woman drunken with the blood of the saints, and with the blood of the martyrs of Jesus. And when I saw her, I wondered with a great wonder.

Rev 17:7 And the angel said unto me, Wherefore didst thou wonder? I will tell thee the mystery of the woman, and of the beast that carrieth her, which hath the seven heads and the ten horns.

Rev 17:8 The beast that thou sawest was, and is not; and is about to come up out of the abyss, and to go into perdition. And they that dwell on the earth shall wonder, they whose name hath not been written in the book of life from the foundation of the world, when they behold the beast, how that he was, and is not, and shall come.

Rev 17:9 Here is the mind that hath wisdom. The seven heads are seven mountains, on which the woman sitteth:

Rev 17:10 and they are seven kings; the five are fallen, the one is, the other is not yet come; and when he cometh, he must continue a little while.

Rev 17:11 And the beast that was, and is not, is himself also an eighth, and is of the seven; and he goeth into perdition.

Rev 17:12 And the ten horns that thou sawest are ten kings, who have received no kingdom as yet; but they receive authority as kings, with the beast, for one hour.

Rev 17:13 These have one mind, and they give their power and authority unto the beast.

Rev 17:14 These shall war against the Lamb, and the Lamb shall overcome them, for he is Lord of lords, and King of kings; and they also shall overcome that are with him, called and chosen and faithful.

Rev 17:15 And he saith unto me, The waters which thou sawest, where the harlot sitteth, are peoples, and multitudes, and nations, and tongues.

Rev 17:16 And the ten horns which thou sawest, and the beast, these shall hate the harlot, and shall make her desolate and naked, and shall eat her flesh, and shall burn her utterly with fire.

Rev 17:17 For God did put in their hearts to do his mind, and to come to one mind, and to give their kingdom unto the beast, until the words of God should be accomplished.

Rev 17:18 And the woman whom thou sawest is the great city, which reigneth over the kings of the earth.

Chapter 17 verse 1 says, "one of the seven angels *that had*, (past tense), the seven bowls." Thus by determining the time frame of chapter 17, a lot can be known about the time relationship between the trumpet and bowl judgments. By this revealing presentation of chapter 17 verse 1, 6 of the 7 angels having the 7 bowls now have empty bowls. The angel of verse 1 would be one of the six with an empty bowls. One angel at this time point will still have a full bowl that of course is the 7th angel who will pour out that bowl just before the 2nd coming, which will occur about one year later in time. This is further proof that the bowl judgments could not follow the trumpet judgments as by this wording the 7 trumpet will be sounded after this time point, just before the 2nd coming which is about 12 months after this event. Clearly, bowl judgments will be poured out before the time occurrence of chapter 17 verses 1. All is making perfect sense.

Chapter 17 involves the copycat church. At the time the true church is rapture into heaven, there will remain occult churches and members who will not make the trip as they deny our Lord Jesus Christ. These groups perhaps use His name or even acknowledge His life, but, will deny the power thereof. These groups will not accept our Lord Jesus

Christ as their personal Savior. These groups will become the church of Satan. These groups will support the things of Satan as they are a worldly group. Occult church groups can be defined by the following definition; "a group who attempts to put Jesus Christ on an elevator and bring Him downstairs." Satan for a time will put up with this group, but, will grow cold to this group and turn against and destroy them.

Are you confused by the meaning of the 10 horns and 7 heads of both Satan and the beast? Chapter 17 lays out the meaning of these symbols. The 10 horns are 10 persons which will be summand by our Lord; see chapter 17 verses 12-17, to rule over the 200 million man army that will cross the Euphrates River. Seemingly, the beast makes promises to them, perhaps to be rulers over the earth, after he wins the battle with our Lord. Kind of like counting your chickens before they hatch. The 7 heads have a dual meaning. One meaning represents a location, while the 2nd meaning tells of 7 kings. Five of these kings are past tenses which were. One, the sixth king is a little unclear as to the time frame this king will sever. Most likely being a time frame representing John's life, which would mean the 6th king could be referring to Domitian. The 7th head or 7th king is the person who will sign the 7 year covenant agreement with the Nation of Israel. Although Paul says this person will be revealed and tells us that 3 times. No one today can tell us the name of this person. Those making the assertion that things of Dan 9:27 and of Revelation happened around 70 A.D. is just beyond reason with many scriptures and history refuting that claim. All call the person who will sign an agreement with Israel the antichrist and that is at least who he becomes but no one refers to this person as the 7th king. That 7th king will rule for a little while which is 3-1/2 years, the 1st 3-1/2 years of the 7 years making up the hour of trail or testing, listed in Rev 3:10. Then he undergoes a change giving himself to the spirit of Satan becoming an 8th king, the beast. This person until the breaking of the 7 year agreement is not particularly a Satanic driven person, but, is a very worldly person. This person becomes a Satanic driven person at or after the 7 year agreement is broken when this person gives himself to Satan and is indwelled by the spirit of Satan. Satan is the great deceiver, and likely deceives the 7th king with false promises concerning the takeover of the universe. The 7th king, now the 8th king falls for the deception hook line and sinker.

Chapter 17 verse 11 tells that this person, the 7th king, becomes the beast the 8th king. Now armed with this false promise the 8th king, the beast with his promise in hand, turns to the 10 persons ruling the 200 million man army and offers them kingships based upon the deception form Satan to the beast. Now we can perhaps place this understanding to work in our everyday lives.

This information along with the realization that the Nation of Israel will only sign an agreement with a person in a very high worldly ranking order, means that if the time is close, we perhaps should be looking for this 7th king, who will likely be the ruler of a nation or group of nations, possessing nuclear weapons. In order for this person to pursue the Jewish peoples over the entire world means the ability to pursue would need to be there. The ability to pursue will be by military force.

Being it is given that the pursuit will be by means of war and we know the length of time which will be just 3-1/2 years, which is a very short time period; nuclear weapons are the only means known that could produce the amount of carnage that is to come upon this world. To point out, in just 3-1/2 years 3.6 – 4 billion people will lose their lives. That number perhaps will be even larger as we simply do not know nor can we know the exact number. The 60 million killed during all of WWII is only about 0.015% of those who we are told will be killed. Our Lord says in Mat 24:22, "and except those days had been shortened, no flesh would have been saved: but for the *elect's sake* those days shall be shortened." Note that it says for the *elect's sake*. This means that only saved persons will enter into the millennial 1000 year reign directly from the great tribulation. More will be given about that later.

We should remember that the book of Revelation calls itself prophecy. Will there be supernatural intervention that just strikes people dead without the use of nuclear weapons? First of all, we know our Lord Jesus Christ has unlimited powers and could do that if it were His choosing, however, past fulfilled prophecy likely would provide for us the clearer picture of things to come. The prophecies of Jeremiah, Ezekiel, and Daniel, about the destruction of Jerusalem and the temple, came about as they predicted without supernatural intervention, at least in a direct way. It is likely that the prophecies concerning the things of Revelation will be fulfilled by the actions of man directed by spiritual powers. Perhaps looking at spiritual power at work will help us understand. In the following verse we see that God will be directing the affairs of men by controlling their minds. Yet it will be the physical actions of man that will render the deeds of Revelation. During the 2nd coming, supernatural powers will be used as our Lord will as listed in the verses of chapter 19, personally destroy His foes at the battle of Armageddon.

Rev 17:17 *For God has put it into their hearts to carry out His plan by having one purpose and to give their kingdom to the beast until God's words are accomplished.*

Will the United States be involved in the great tribulation to come? As previously stated, the United States has a Jewish population numbering to that of the Nation of Israel or perhaps greater than that of Israel. Therefore, there is no conceived way the United States can sit on the side lines. The great tribulation will be a true worldwide affair.

No suggestion is given that the time is close as this author does not possess that knowledge. Mat 24:36 informs us that no one has this information except our heavenly Father, yet we can and should know when the season is at hand. That knowledge can be gain through Matthew chapter 24; Mark chapter 13; and Luke chapter 21.

Time frame for charting of these events is around one year before the 2nd coming. Not an exact time placement. The events of chapter 17 are known to follow the Euphrates River crossing. That crossing will occur about 13 months before the 2nd coming. The reason chapter 17 is known to follow the river crossing is the listing of the ten kings in chapter 17:12-14. These same 10 kings are the commanders of the 200 million man army that will cross the Euphrates River.

Chapter 18

Is a complete chapter with no splitting of its verses, Babylon the great has fallen

Rev 18:1 After these things I saw another angel coming down out of heaven, having great authority; and the earth was lightened with his glory. Rev 18:2 And he cried with a mighty voice, saying, ***Fallen, fallen is Babylon the grea***t, and is become a habitation of demons, and a hold of every unclean spirit, and a hold of every unclean and hateful bird. Rev 18:3 For by the wine of the wrath of her fornication all the nations are fallen; and the kings of the earth committed fornication with her, and the merchants of the earth waxed rich by the power of her wantonness. Rev 18:4 And I heard another voice from heaven, saying, Come forth, my people, out of her, that ye have no fellowship with her sins, and that ye receive not of her plagues:

In chapter 14 verses 6-8 angels call to those on the earth to come to salvation. In chapter 18 verse 4 the saying, Come forth, my people, is that call. How could the call be in chapter 14, when some of those called are in chapter 18? The answer is coming as we will soon see the correct placement for chapter 14. Following is the call to salvation made from chapter 14.

Rev 14:6 *And I saw another angel flying in mid heaven, having eternal good tidings to proclaim unto them that dwell on the earth, and unto every nation and tribe and tongue and people;*
Rev 14:7 *and he saith with a great voice, Fear God, and give him glory; for the hour of his judgment is come: and worship him that made the heaven and the earth and sea and fountains of waters.*
Rev 14:8 *And another, a second angel, followed, saying, **Fallen, fallen is Babylon the great**, that hath made all the nations to drink of the wine of the wrath of her fornication.*

Rev 18:5 for her sins have reached even unto heaven, and God hath remembered her iniquities.
Rev 18:6 Render unto her even as she rendered, and double unto her the

double according to her works: in the cup which she mingled, mingle unto her double.

Rev 18:7 How much soever she glorified herself, and waxed wanton, so much give her of torment and mourning: for she saith in her heart, I sit a queen, and am no widow, and shall in no wise see mourning.

Rev 18:8 Therefore in one day shall her plagues come, death, and mourning, and famine; and she shall be utterly burned with fire; for strong is the Lord God who judged her.

Rev 18:9 And the kings of the earth, who committed fornication and lived wantonly with her, shall weep and wail over her, when they look upon the smoke of her burning,

Rev 18:10 standing afar off for the fear of her torment, saying, Woe, woe, the great city, Babylon, the strong city! for in one hour is thy judgment come.

Rev 18:11 And the merchants of the earth weep and mourn over her, for no man buyeth their merchandise any more;

Rev 18:12 merchandise of gold, and silver, and precious stone, and pearls, and fine linen, and purple, and silk, and scarlet; and all thyine wood, and every vessel of ivory, and every vessel made of most precious wood, and of brass, and iron, and marble;

Rev 18:13 and cinnamon, and spice, and incense, and ointment, and frankincense, and wine, and oil, and fine flour, and wheat, and cattle, and sheep; and merchandise of horses and chariots and slaves; and souls of men.

Rev 18:14 And the fruits which thy soul lusted after are gone from thee, and all things that were dainty and sumptuous are perished from thee, and men shall find them no more at all.

Rev 18:15 The merchants of these things, who were made rich by her, shall stand afar off for the fear of her torment, weeping and mourning;

Rev 18:16 saying, Woe, woe, the great city, she that was arrayed in fine linen and purple and scarlet, and decked with gold and precious stone and pearl!

Rev 18:17 for in an hour so great riches is made desolate. And every shipmaster, and every one that saileth any wither, and mariners, and as many as gain their living by sea, stood afar off,

Rev 18:18 and cried out as they looked upon the smoke of her burning, saying, What city is like the great city?

Rev 18:19 And they cast dust on their heads, and cried, weeping and mourning, saying, Woe, woe, the great city, wherein all that had their ships in the sea were made rich by reason of her costliness! for in one hour is she made desolate.

Rev 18:20 Rejoice over her, thou heaven, and ye saints, and ye apostles, and ye prophets; for God hath judged your judgment on her.

Rev 18:21 And a strong angel took up a stone as it were a great millstone and cast it into the sea, saying, Thus with a mighty fall shall Babylon, the great city, be cast down, and shall be found no more at all.

Rev 18:22 And the voice of harpers and minstrels and flute-players and trumpeters shall be heard no more at all in thee; and no craftsman, of whatsoever craft, shall be found any more at all in thee; and the voice of a mill shall be heard no more at all in thee;

Rev 18:23 and the light of a lamp shall shine no more at all in thee; and the voice of the bridegroom and of the bride shall be heard no more at all in thee: for thy merchants were the princes of the earth; for with thy sorcery were all the nations deceived.

Rev 18:24 And in her was found the blood of prophets and of saints, and of all that have been slain upon the earth.

A revealing is in order that to the knowledge of this earthly author only occurs within the pages of the book of Revelation. Revealed is the path the Master Author, our Lord Jesus Christ used to display His path and method used for the correct placement of chapter 14. The original manuscripts assuredly do contain this information; this is not an itching ear teaching. All information given here is in your Bible versions, which you should check. This information has been there from the time of pinning over 1900 years ago. Words vary from Bible version to Bible version. However, all versions checked contain this information. Before listing this path information please consider the following.

Rev 22:18 *I testify unto every man that heareth the words of the prophecy of this book, if any man shall add unto them, God shall add unto him the plagues which are written in this book:*

Rev 22:19 *and if any man shall take away from the words of the book of this prophecy, God shall take away his part from the tree of life, and out of the holy city, which are written in this book.*

Chapter 22 verses 18 and 19 contains a warning to all not to add to nor take away from the words of this prophecy. Nothing, in this revealing, adds or takes away from the words of Revelation. Although to this point in writing there are verses from chapter 7 and chapter 11 which have not been included as of yet, those verses are not forgotten and will be included at their appropriate times.

Chapter 14 has been a skipped over chapter. The reason for that is that chapter 14 does not belong in its numeric order. The identifiers of proper placement for chapter 14 have always been included in the scripture writings of Revelation. Man has not recognized their existence. Our Lord hid in plain sight for over 1900 years His directions for the proper placement of chapter 14.

Our Lord provided information to allow all to know the proper placement of chapter 14 by providing like _word phrases_. The original manuscripts do not contain chapter and verse designations, but, do include like _word phrases_. Chapter and verses designations were added during the 1300th century. That of course was at least 1200 years after the original writing.

Now please consider the following;

Rev 18:2 And he cried with a mighty voice, saying, _**Fallen, fallen is Babylon the great**_, and is become a habitation of demons, and a hold of every unclean spirit, and a hold of every unclean and hateful bird.

Rev 14:8 And another, a second angel, followed, saying, _**Fallen, fallen is Babylon the great**_, that hath made all the nations to drink of the wine of the wrath of her fornication.

Rev 19:6 And I heard as it were the voice of a great multitude, and _**as the voice of many waters, and as the voice of mighty thunders**_, saying, Hallelujah: for the Lord our God, the Almighty, reigneth.

Rev 14:2 And I heard a voice from heaven, _**as the voice of many waters, and as the voice of a great thunder**_: and the voice which I heard was as the voice of harpers harping with their harps:

A question for you. If you worked on a car parking lot and your boss told you to park a particular vehicle between AA and BB, do you think you could do the job? If you purchased furniture from IKEA which is knocked down and in a box of pieces with numbers or letter directing the position of each furniture piece, do you think you could assemble the furniture? Do you think our Lord is telling us to park chapter 14 between chapters 18 and 19? If not, please explain to all; these _word phrases._

If the like _word phrases_ are not enough, check out the contents of chapter 14 and compare the contents with chapters 13 and 15. Then compare chapter 14 contents with chapters 18 and 19. Subject matter does matter and should run from one chapter into the following chapter. All should realize that Babylon is not the subject matter of chapter 14. Babylon will not fall until chapter 18, so how could Babylon be listed as fallen in chapter 14, which would be the case if chapter 14 were placed in its numeric position between chapters 13 and 15?

Our Lord knew that no intelligible meaning could be made of the book of Revelation without the proper placement of chapter 14. Misunderstanding and manufacturing of man's paths, have stood in for intelligible understanding. We will see that chapter 14 placed between chapters 18 and 19 conveys perfect sense. We will see that happenings of chapter 14 make sense when coupled with the events, particularly, of chapter 19.

For over 1900 years many eyes have seen without understanding. Hidden in plain sight to fulfill His reasons. Are there scriptures to support His hiding, or His control of man's mind?

Please read Rev 17:17 For God did put in their hearts to do his mind, and to come to one mind, and to give their kingdom unto the beast, until the words of God should be accomplished. Several other scriptures could be sighted. Could our God blind our minds so we could not see what was right in front of us? Could our God after hiding right in front of us for over 1900 years now uncover to allow us to see?

Many searches have been performed searching for knowledge of these _word phrases_. No information was found involving like _word phrases_. As it appears that no one knows about them.

Our Lord, by necessity, would have had to be the reason for the inclusion of these _word phrases_. Why did He use this method and why is He revealing this now? Although this earthly author has been given the answers to many things concerning the book of Revelation, His reasons for using _word phrases_ and revealing now was not given. To this earthly author the placement of these _word phrases_ is more than enough to convince, that these phrases are not a coincidence, they are not accidental, and that they represent the method used by the creator of the universe to fulfill His plan. Listed so far are part of the _word phrases_ used. Others remain to be listed at their appropriate times.

Chapter 14 verses 1-13

With its exact _word phrase_ matches with chapters 18 and 19;
Chapter 14, is a split chapter split three times,
Chapter 14 is a chapter that does not belong in its numeric assignment.

Rev 14:1 And I saw, and behold, the Lamb standing on the mount Zion, and with him a hundred and forty and four thousand, having his name, and the name of his Father, written on their foreheads.

Chapter 14 has confounded many a person trying to make sense of the book of Revelation. Mostly, that confusion is due to not realizing that chapter 14 does not belong between chapters 13 and 15, as one would normally expect. This should have been realized as it is clear by the listed 42 months of Rev 13:5. Because of that listing the precise placement of chapter 13 can be made on a time scale representing the 7 year tribulation time period. That precise position is at the very beginning of the 2nd 3-1/2 year time period. If chapter 14 followed chapter 13 as normal then the time frame for chapter 14 would have occurred in the very early part of the great tribulation. Meaning that the 144,000 sealed would only be on earth for perhaps a couple of months before they would be rapture into heaven. These facts should have served as a red flag for all to see, however, all missed this realization.

Rev 14:2 And I heard a voice from heaven, _**as the voice of many waters, and as the voice of a great thunder:**_ and the voice which I heard was as the voice of harpers harping with their harps:
Rev 14:3 and they sing as it were a new song before the throne, and before the four living creatures and the elders: and no man could learn the song save the hundred and forty and four thousand, even they that had been purchased out of the earth.
Rev 14:4 These are they that were not defiled with women; for they are virgins. These are they that follow the Lamb whithersoever he goeth. These were purchased from among men, to be the firstfruits unto God and

unto the Lamb.

Rev 14:5 And in their mouth was found no lie: they are without blemish.

Rev 14:6 And I saw another angel flying in mid heaven, having eternal good tidings to proclaim unto them that dwell on the earth, and unto every nation and tribe and tongue and people;

Rev 14:7 and he saith with a great voice, Fear God, and give him glory; for the hour of his judgment is come: and worship him that made the heaven and the earth and sea and fountains of waters.

Rev 14:8 And another, a second angel, followed, saying, ***Fallen, fallen is Babylon the great,*** that hath made all the nations to drink of the wine of the wrath of her fornication.

Rev 14:9 And another angel, a third, followed them, saying with a great voice, If any man worshippeth the beast and his image, and receiveth a mark on his forehead, or upon his hand,

Rev 14:10 he also shall drink of the wine of the wrath of God, which is prepared unmixed in the cup of his anger; and he shall be tormented with fire and brimstone in the presence of the holy angels, and in the presence of the Lamb:

Rev 14:11 and the smoke of their torment goeth up for ever and ever; and they have no rest day and night, they that worship the beast and his image, and whoso receiveth the mark of his name.

Rev 14:12 Here is the patience of the saints, they that keep the commandments of God, and the faith of Jesus.

Rev 14:13 And I heard the voice from heaven saying, Write, Blessed are the dead who die in the Lord from henceforth: yea, saith the Spirit, that they may rest from their labors; for their works follow with them.

Chapter 7 verses 9-17

2nd martyred group in heaven
Chapter 7 is a split chapter, split two times.
The 1st part has been listed,
The 2nd part will receive it's time placement.

How is it known that chapter 7 verses 9-17 belong in the 2nd 3-1/2 year time frame? In chapter 7 verse 13 John is asked by an elder, where did these people come from? In chapter 7 verse 14 John responds by saying I don't know, you know. The elder then tells John, these come out of the great tribulation.

Remember that the great tribulation was found to be the 2nd or last 3-1/2 year time period which will make up the 7 years of the hour of testing, Rev 3:10. It was found that Mat 24:21 shares the same subject matter with Mat 24:15. The event in Mat 24:15, will take place at the start of the 2nd 3-1/2 year time period as listed in Dan 9:27. Again the 2nd 3-1/2 years is the time period of the great tribulation.

Now we will see the importance of knowing that the great tribulation is the last 3-1/2 years of the 7 year time period known as the hour of testing. If the great tribulation involved the full 7 year time period, we would not be able to use the designation, found in verse 14, to identify the time placement of chapter 7 verses 9-17 as being apart from chapter 7 verses 1-8. Armed with the understanding that the great tribulation is the 2nd or the last 3-1/2 years we know that chapter 7 verses 9-17 belongs somewhere in that time frame.

That is great information and does narrow down for us a great deal the time placement, but, we need a way of _precisely_ placing this chapter and its verses within the 2nd 3-1/2 year time period. Our Lord provided for us that farther narrowing, He provided an exact _word phrase_, to allow us to know the precise placement within this 3-1/2 year. Chapter 7 verse 9 holds that narrowing information. We see the _word phrase_, "_great multitude_." This exact _word phrase_ is also found in chapter 19 verses 1 and 6. This term, *great multitude*, is found three times in the entire Bible. Some Bible versions use the term, vast multitude. Note: that the term is not a derived from the apostle John, as that term is not used in any of John's other writings. This term was given to John by our Lord Jesus Christ as a tool for you and I to use. By examination, it is found that chapter 7 verse 9, and chapter 19 verses 1 and 6 are all describing the same group. In fact chapter 7 verse 9 holds defining information that chapter 19 verses 1 and 6 do not hold. In other words this term is not describing three groups; the three terms are describing one group.

Therefore, these three listings are a group and should appear as a grouping. Thus chapter 7 verses 9-17, belongs just before the listing of chapter 19 verses 1-10. That is the charting position for chapter 7 verses 9-17. Further chapter 7 verses 1-8 time frame is not a part of the great tribulation time period as those verses represent a time period just before the start of the great tribulation and are in the 1st 3-1/2 year time period, at the very end of that time period. Thus we should realize that verses 1-8 will occur in the 1st 3-1/2 years while verse 9-17 will occur in the 2nd 3-1/2 years.

This is absolute proof of split chapters within the book of Revelation. Split chapters carry a relationship with time gaps. Remember from chapter 12 verse 5, which is a time gap, that verse contains three time periods. Remember also that time gaps are not unusual in the Bible. Split chapters use multiple verses representing a time period, where a time gap has multiple time periods within one verse. The difference is in the length of the description. This information should help in the study of the whole Bible.

Who are those of the great multitude? That group is made up of all saved persons who will die during the 2nd 3-1/2 years, the great tribulation. Does this group contain the church group? NO! The church group will be raptured into heaven over 3-1/2 years before the first person will die which make up this group. We should remember the 5th seal judgment. Those appearing in heaven that were given white robes and told to wait until others join them that would be killed as they were. That group will be a part of this great multitude as they came out of the great tribulation.

We are told that the size of this group is so large that no man could number. From chapter 7 verse 9 we see that the makeup of this group will be from all over the entire world, containing both Jewish and non-Jewish persons. Their only requirement for being in the present heaven is given in chapter 7 verse 14, *they washed their robes, and made them white in the blood of the Lamb*.

How does this group find its way into heaven? They don't. They are raptured, they are taken, into the present heaven. With all taken into heaven, the power of the actions lay with our Lord Jesus Christ. We know this group arrives by at least two different raptures, yet, we cannot be certain of the rapture number. We know the 5th seal group to be one rapture while the remainder is from a second rapture later in time during the great tribulation. The 5th seal judgment group died as a result of the 2nd, 3rd, and 4th seal judgments.

A second group will die as a result of the 200 million man army that will cross the Euphrates River, about 13 months before the 2nd coming. We see that information coming to us out of chapter 9 verse18. The earth's population will be reduced by one fourth due to the 2nd, 3rd, and 4th seal judgments. Those actions will take place around the second month to the sixth month of the great tribulation. Please do not make too much of the given time assignments, as some cannot be precisely positioned as that information is just not given. Time assignments are given to allow all to see a relative relationship of events.

In chapter 9 verse 18 we are told that a third of the remaining earth's population will be killed. That figure again will be around 1.8 billion people. How can we wrap our mental arms around such a number? That amount of people more than equals all persons living in North, South, and Central America, which has a listing of about 1 billion people. Chapter 7 verse 9 says, concerning the size of that group, which no man could number; perhaps we should just leave it at that.

Rev 7:9 After these things I saw, and behold, a ***great multitude***, which no man could number, out of every nation and of all tribes and peoples and tongues, standing before the throne and before the Lamb, arrayed in white robes, and palms in their hands;

Rev 7:10 and they cry with a great voice, saying, Salvation unto our God who sitteth on the throne, and unto the Lamb.

Rev 7:11 And all the angels were standing round about the throne, and about the elders and the four living creatures; and they fell before the throne on their faces, and worshipped God,

Rev 7:12 saying, Amen: Blessing, and glory, and wisdom, and thanksgiving, and honor, and power, and might, be unto our God for ever and ever. Amen.

Rev 7:13 And one of the elders answered, saying unto me, These that are arrayed in white robes, who are they, and whence came they?

Rev 7:14 And I say unto him, My lord, thou knowest. And he said to me, These are they that come of the **_great tribulation_**, and they washed their robes, and made them white in the blood of the Lamb.

Rev 7:15 Therefore are they before the throne of God; and they serve him day and night in his temple: and he that sitteth on the throne shall spread his tabernacle over them.

Rev 7:16 They shall hunger no more, neither thirst any more; neither shall the sun strike upon them, nor any heat:

Rev 7:17 for the Lamb that is in the midst of the throne shall be their shepherd, and shall guide them unto fountains of waters of life: and God shall wipe away every tear from their eyes. Please read chapter 21 and 22.

Chapter 19 verses 1-10

The various groups in heaven
The marriage of the Lamb
Chapter 19 is a split chapter- split three times

Rev 19:1 After these things I heard as it were a great voice of a ***great multitude*** in heaven, saying, Hallelujah; Salvation, and glory, and power, belong to our God:

Rev 19:2 for true and righteous are his judgments; for he hath judged the great harlot, her that corrupted the earth with her fornication, and he hath avenged the blood of his servants at her hand.

Rev 19:3 And a second time they say, Hallelujah. And her smoke goeth up for ever and ever.

Rev 19:4 And the four and twenty elders and the four living creatures fell down and worshipped God that sitteth on the throne, saying, Amen; Hallelujah.

Rev 19:5 And a voice came forth from the throne, saying, Give praise to our God, all ye his servants, ye that fear him, the small and the great.

Rev 19:6 And I heard as it were the voice of a ***great multitude,*** and ***as the voice of many waters, and as the voice of mighty thunders,*** saying, Hallelujah: for the Lord our God, the Almighty, reigneth.

Rev 19:7 Let us rejoice and be exceeding glad, and let us give the glory unto him: for the marriage of the Lamb is come, and his wife hath made herself ready.

Rev 19:8 And it was given unto her that she should array herself in fine linen, bright and pure: for the fine linen is the righteous acts of the saints.

Rev 19:9 And he saith unto me, Write, Blessed are they that are bidden to the marriage supper of the Lamb. And he saith unto me, These are true words of God.

Rev 19:10 And I fell down before his feet to worship him. And he saith unto me, See thou do it not: I am a fellow-servant with thee and with thy brethren that hold the testimony of Jesus: worship God; for the testimony of Jesus is the spirit of prophecy.

In chapter 19 verses 1-10 are seen the presents of all human beings in the present heaven from all times past. The present time frame is a time just before the 2nd coming. Nothing tells us how much time before the 2nd coming that the events of verses 1-10 will take place, yet likely it is just a few days. Some groups present are listed by groups while others are known to be there by descriptions.

1. We know the great multitude group are those from the great tribulation time period as we are clearly given that information in chapter 7 verse 14.
2. We clearly see the 24 elders as being present listed in verse 4. The 24 elders are listed six times from chapter 4 onward.
3. We see that the four living creatures are also in attendance.
4. In verse 5 we see the phrase, "*all ye his servants, ye that fear him, the small and the great.*" That statement is an indication that other groups are present. We see that indication again in verse 6 when the statement made seems to be directed to three distinct groups. We read, ^{1st} *the voice of a great multitude,*^{2nd} *and as the voice of many waters,* ^{3rd} *and as the voice of mighty thunders*
5. By verse 7 we know the church group is there. The church group is the bride of the Lamb. Presumably, the church group is either the *voice of many waters, or the voice of a mighty thunder.*
6. We know from the descriptions given that the church group is present and will be the bride of the Lamb, and we know that other groups are present that will not be the bride of the Lamb, but, we are told these groups are blessed to have been called to the marriage of the Lamb.

Certainly, it is a blessing to be called a child of God. What a blessing it will be to be the bride of the Lamb. This ceremony, this marriage, would have to be held in heaven as likely there would be no one place on earth with captive to accommodate such a huge number of persons. The time period for charting purposes is immediately before the 2nd coming. Likely a matter of days before the 2nd coming.

Please note; that chapter 19 verse 2 says the judgment has been carried out. This is speaking of Babylon. Please note that Chapter 14 verse 8 says the judgment has been carried out. Please note that Chapter 18 verse 2 says the judgment has been carried out, while chapter 17 tells of the events leading up to the judgment. Therefore, chapter 14, by this subject matter, must follow chapter 18 verse 2. This of course agrees with the _word phrase_ matches and most importantly matches what this earthly author was shown by the Spirit of the Lord.

Indeed, without the understanding involving the placement of chapter 14, no intelligible meaning can be made of Revelation. The placement of chapter 14 has not been realized in the past. That reason has lead to man's creative mind spinning a large assortment of paths. We are going to see further connections of chapter 14 to chapter 19. But first we must deal with the connection of the second split chapter, chapter 11.

Chapter 11 verses 7-14

Calling home of the two witnesses, rapture.
Chapter 11 is a split chapter, split three times.

How is it known that the 2 witnesses will serve in the great tribulation time period? We are clearly given that information in chapter 11 verse 3. The length of time listed in verse 3 is 1260 days which equals 3-1/2 years. The 7 year time period is divided into (2), 3-1/2 time periods by the event of Mat 24:15. That event, the defilement of the temple, will take place in the middle of the 7 year time period. Verse 2 speaks of the defilement of the temple as only Jewish persons are allowed on the temple mount. Please do understanding this constitutes a parcel defilement. With the listing of this defilement, we know verse 2 is at the very beginning of the 2nd 3-1/2 year time period called the great tribulation. Verse 3 then gives us the length of time these 2 witnesses will sever which is 1260 days or 3-1/2 years. We do not have to guess as some have done, we have His provided Words, allowing precise time placement. By verse 3 and the length of time listed there, we know that verses 7-14 will occur at the very end of the great tribulation time period, just before the 2nd coming. Remember that the 2nd coming is the closing event of the 7 year time period. Therefore we can precisely place the ending events of the 2 witnesses just before the 2nd coming of our Lord Jesus Christ. Like a bus driver waiting for 2 men running to catch the bus just before leaving, perhaps we can see in our minds our Lord Jesus Christ calling out to these 2 witnesses, "hurry boys, the horses are impatient and wanting to leave." The importance of using a dry erase board should be clearly seen. A popular TV minister contends these two witnesses will witness in the 1st 3-1/2 years. That error is due to a strict chronological reading of Revelation which results in misunderstanding. When one event is misunderstood, misunderstandings, multiples creating multiple errors, culminating in total confusion. No longer should the condition of confusion exist for all reading at this point should have a clear understanding that the book of Revelation is as a *fact* out of chronological order from chapter 6 through chapter 19.

Rev 11:7 And when they shall have finished their testimony, the beast that cometh up out of the abyss shall make war with them, and overcome them, and kill them.

Rev 11:8 And their dead bodies lie in the street of the great city, which spiritually is called Sodom and Egypt, where also their Lord was crucified.

Rev 11:9 And from among the peoples and tribes and tongues and nations do men look upon their dead bodies three days and a half, and suffer not their dead bodies to be laid in a tomb.

Rev 11:10 And they that dwell on the earth rejoice over them, and make merry; and they shall send gifts one to another; because these two prophets tormented them that dwell on the earth.

Rev 11:11 And after the three days and a half the breath of life from God entered into them, and they stood upon their feet; and great fear fell upon them that beheld them.

Rev 11:12 And they heard a great voice from heaven saying unto them, Come up hither. And they went up into heaven in the cloud; and their enemies beheld them.

Rev 11:13 And in that hour there was a great earthquake, and the tenth part of the city fell; and there were killed in the earthquake seven thousand persons: and the rest were affrighted, and gave glory to the God of heaven.

Rev 11:14 The second Woe is past: behold, the third Woe cometh quickly.

The two witnesses called by God to witness to the Nation of Israel will witness from their bases of operation being the City of Jerusalem. Satan and the beast will not like their message and will attempt to stop their witnessing. The 2 witnesses are allowed to protect themselves with fire from their mouths until their job is done. These witnesses will be involved with the administering of the trumpet and bowl judgments. Their finger prints can be seen all over these judgments. They will not be involved in the seal judgments as only our Lord Jesus Christ was found worthy of that task. Seen in chapter 16 verse 12 the sixth bowl judgment, the waters of the Euphrates River will be dried up to allow the 200 million man army an easier crossing. Rain fall will be stopped to provide this condition. The two witnesses have the ability to stop rain fall.

Likely, we will know, as a future event, the number of persons that will accept Jesus Christ as their Messiah and Savior as a result of these two witnesses. After their tour of duty which we know will last for 3-1/2

years, their protection will be taken away and they will be allowed to be killed and their bodies will lie in the street for 3-1/2 days. Life will be given to their bodies and they will be called into heaven, yet another rapture, and then they will be members of the armies of heaven, mounting white horses making the trip back to this present earth.

At the time of the 2nd coming, another time period is seen where a stacking effect will happen. In a short period of time there will be the occurrences of many events. Charting will help with understanding.

Chapter 16 verses 17-21

Rev 16:17 And the seventh poured out his bowl upon the air; and there came forth a great voice out of the temple, from the throne, saying, It is done:

The saying, "it is done," would that not be the same thing as; then is finished the mystery of God, listed as part of the 7th trumpet? The 7th bowl judgment will be administered immediately before the sounding of the 7th trumpet judgment.

Rev 15:8 *And the temple was filled with smoke from the glory of God, and from his power; and none was able to enter into the temple, till the seven plagues of the seven angels should be finished.*

We clearly see the temple reopened in chapter 11 verse 19. By that provided information we can and do know the time order involving both the 7th bowl and 7th trumpet judgments. The time gap between the 7th bowl and 7th trumpet likely will be minuscule, separated by no measurable time. That is likely the conditions involving the calling home of the two witnesses, the 7th bowl and the 7th trumpet judgments. All three events likely would seem like one event if we stood and watched their administering.

Rev 16:18 and there were lightnings, and voices, and thunders; and there was a great earthquake, such as was not since there were men upon the earth, so great an earthquake, so mighty.

Rev 16:19 And the great city was divided into three parts, and the cities of the nations fell: and Babylon the great was remembered in the sight of God, to give unto her the cup of the wine of the fierceness of his wrath. Rev 16:20 And every island fled away, and the mountains were not found. Rev 16:21 And great hail, every stone about the weight of a talent, cometh down out of heaven upon men: and men blasphemed God because of the plague of the hail; for the plague thereof is exceeding great.

Chapter 11 verses 15-19

The sounding of the 7th trumpet
Chapter 11 is a split chapter

Rev 11:15 And the seventh angel sounded; and there followed great voices in heaven, and they said, The kingdom of the world is become the kingdom of our Lord, and of his Christ: and he shall reign for ever and ever.

How much clearer could our Lord say to us, "the 2nd coming is here?

Rev 10:7 *but in the days of the voice of the seventh angel, when he is about to sound, then is finished the mystery of God, according to the good tidings which he declared to his servants the prophets.*

Rev 11:16 And the four and twenty elders, who sit before God on their thrones, fell upon their faces and worshipped God,
Rev 11:17 saying, We give thee thanks, O Lord God, the Almighty, who art and who wast; because thou hast taken thy great power, and didst reign. Rev 11:18 ^{1st} And the nations were wroth, and thy wrath came, ^{2nd} and the time of the dead to be judged, and the time to give their reward to thy servants the prophets, and to the saints, and to them that fear thy name, the small and the great; ^{3rd} and to destroy them that destroy the earth.

Chapter 11 verse 18 is a time gap with three time periods, the 1st time period will take place before the 2nd coming, and reads as follows; ^{1st}*And the nations were wroth, and thy wrath came,* the 2nd and 3rd time periods jump ahead of time into the millennial reign of Jesus Christ. What chapter 11 verse 18 is describing in the 2nd and 3rd time gaps is

the 1st and 2nd resurrections, listed after the 1st comma; ^{2nd} *and the time of the dead to be judged, and the time to give their reward to thy servants the prophets, and to the saints, and to them that fear thy name, the small and the great*; those are the actions of chapter 20 verses 4-6, that is the first resurrection. Listed after the fourth comma is the 3rd time gap; ^{3rd} *and to destroy them that destroy the earth.* This action will be taken during the 2nd resurrection, the great white throne judgment seat which will happen 1000 years after the first resurrection. Those actions are listed for us in chapter 20 verses 11-15. When we read in chapter 20 verses 4-6 we are reading the fulfillment of the events listed in chapter 11 verse 18, the 2nd part. When we read in chapter 20 verses 11-15, we are reading the fulfillment of chapter 11 verse 18, the 3rd part. This illustration should bring home the importance of understanding time gaps. Remember time gaps occur all over the entire Bible. Also realize the compounding of misunderstanding if chapter 11 was not recognized as a split chapter and all of chapter 11 was applied in the middle of the 7 years time period, a time period 3-1/2 years earlier. Most say they are confused by Revelation, can we see why?

Many believe the 24 elders are representative of the church group. The fact that chapter 11 verse 18 seems to be all inclusive and uses the word *saints* to describe those who will take part in the rewards to be handed out during the millennial reign described in chapter 20 verses 4-6, seems to cause a problem with the 24 elders being the church group. From the very 1st mention of the 24 elders in chapter 4, it is seen they already have their rewards as they have crowns. It seems for over 2000 years the 24 elders have crowns to cast before the throne. No other group is said to have crowns and no other group is said to cast crowns before the throne, although other groups are said to give praises before the throne. The question should be asked, who are the 24 elders and where and when did they get their crowns? It is obvious there must be more than one rewards time frame. To this earthly author the 24 elders are those our Lord brought with Him when he ascended into heaven after dying on the cross. This group the 24 elders is certainly set apart from the other groups found in heaven through the pages of Revelation. The 24 elders can be ruled out as being prophets as prophets are listed in chapter 11 verse 18 along with *saints*. This is a subject that we may need to *just wait and see, to allow our Lord Jesus Christ to explain to us.*

Rev 20:4 *And I saw thrones, and they sat upon them, and judgment was given unto them: and I saw the souls of them that had been beheaded for the testimony of Jesus, and for the word of God, and such as worshipped not the beast, neither his image, and received not the mark upon their forehead and upon their hand; and they lived, and reigned with Christ a thousand years.*

Rev 20:5 *The rest of the dead lived not until the thousand years should be finished. This is the first resurrection.*

Rev 20:6 *Blessed and holy is he that hath part in the first resurrection: over these the second death hath no power; but they shall be priests of God and of Christ, and shall reign with him a thousand years.*

Rev 20:11 *And I saw a great white throne, and him that sat upon it, from whose face the earth and the heaven fled away; and there was found no place for them.*

Rev 20:12 *And I saw the dead, the great and the small, standing before the throne; and books were opened: and another book was opened, which is the book of life: and the dead were judged out of the things which were written in the books, according to their works.*

Rev 20:13 *And the sea gave up the dead that were in it; and death and Hades gave up the dead that were in them: and they were judged every man according to their works.*

Rev 20:14 *And death and Hades were cast into the lake of fire. This is the second death, even the lake of fire.*

Rev 20:15 *And if any was not found written in the book of life, he was cast into the lake of fire.*

Rev 11:19 And there was opened the temple of God that is in heaven; and there was seen in his temple the ark of his covenant; and there followed lightnings, and voices, and thunders, and an earthquake, and great hail.

Please note the statement of chapter 11 verse 19, which says, "there was opened the temple of God that is in heaven." Now consider the statement of chapter 15 verse 8, which says, "and none was able to enter into the temple, till the seven plagues of the seven angels should be finished." Chapter 11 verse 19 is part of the verses making up the

seventh trumpet judgment. How then could the temple be opened unless the 7th bowl judgment had been administered? Of course the answer is that the 7th bowl judgment will be administered immediately before the 7th trumpet judgment, allowing the reopening of the heavenly temple and the administering of the 7th trumpet judgment, which will occur immediately before the 2nd coming.

At the very end of the great tribulation will be a terrible weather occurrence, with hail stone weighting about 100 pounds each. This will be coupled with the strongest earthquakes this world has ever seen. This will immediately precede the 2nd coming. The piling on effect is seen in the rapture of the two witnesses, in the 7th bowl administering and in the 7th trumpet sounding. The same earthquake is seen in all three events.

Our Lord tells us numerous times that He is coming quickly.

Although the 2nd coming is preceded by several separate events, the time span will be so short that a merging effect in the human mind will be felt, and all these events will seem as one. Charting these events on paper, a dry erase board, caulk board, use what you have, just know that charting will render understanding and understanding is our goal.

Chapter 19 verses 11-16

The blessed event of the 2nd coming,
Chapter 19 is a split chapter;
Events take place inside the confines of the 2nd coming,
Inside that twinkling of an eye.

How fast will the 2nd coming be, at least as fast as the speed of light? That speed; travels at 186,000 miles per second. That is just so many words that do not convey a lot to the human mind. Light would travel seven and one half times around our world, earth, in one second. Another way of saying, "in the twinkling of an eye." For sure we are not talking about a measurable span of time. Click your fingers and it will be done. If you could drive your car at 200 MPH, you would really be moving on, or would you be. How about 760 million MPH, the speed of light? Be sure to change your oil before trying that speed.

Mat 24:27 *For as the lightning cometh forth from the east, and is seen even unto the west; so shall be the coming of the Son of man.*

Rev 19:11 And I saw the heaven opened; and behold, a white horse, and he that sat thereon called Faithful and True; and in righteousness he doth judge and make war.
Rev 19:12 And his eyes are a flame of fire, and upon his head are many diadems; and he hath a name written which no one knoweth but he himself.
Rev 19:13 And he is arrayed in a garment sprinkled with blood: and his name is called The Word of God.
Rev 19:14 And the armies which are in heaven followed him upon white horses, clothed in fine linen, white and pure.
Rev 19:15 And out of his mouth proceedeth a sharp sword, that with it he should smite the nations: and he shall rule them with a rod of iron: *and he treadeth the winepress of the fierceness of the wrath of God, the Almighty.*
Rev 19:16 And he hath on his garment and on his thigh a name written, KINGS OF KINGS, AND LORD OF LORDS.

At this incredible speed, events will take place within that time span. Yes, things will happen within the twinkling of an eye, within the clicking of your fingers. This is not fancy; it is the correct teaching of the Word of God. We now will see another of the important reasons for the correct placement of chapter 14. Verses 14-20 of chapter 14 tell of 2 reaping of the earth. These events will happen inside the twinkling of an eye, something like a plane flying into the eye of a hurricane. The 1st of these 2 reaping is to gather the remaining saved persons from the earth. The call in chapter 18 verse 4 to come forth my people, out of her, is a response of angels witnessing to the entire world found in chapter 14 verses 6 and 7. That witnessing will take place before the 2nd coming. As a result of the angles witnessing listed in chapter 14 verses 6 and 7, many on earth will heed the call and except our Lord Jesus Christ as their Lord and savor. The 2nd reaping is to gather the remaining unsaved persons those rejecting the call of the angels and taking the mark of the beast. The worship of Satan in any form is the unforgiveable sin.

Chapter 14 verses 14-16

The first reaping of the earth, the first gatherings
Chapter 14 is a split chapter; this gathering is not a rapture
Those *gathered* will never see the present heaven.

Chapter 14 verses 14-16 give us an account of the 1st reaping, the 1st gathering of those saved from the earth as a result of the angels witnessing to those on the earth. Likely, that act is the complete fulfillment of the following verse.

Mat 24:14. *And this gospel of the kingdom shall be preached in the whole world for a testimony unto all the nations; and then shall the end come.*

Rev 14:6 And I saw another angel flying in mid heaven, having eternal good tidings to proclaim unto them that dwell on the earth, and unto every nation and tribe and tongue and people;
Rev 14:7 and he saith with a great voice, Fear God, and give him glory; for

the hour of his judgment is come: and worship him that made the heaven and the earth and sea and fountains of waters.

Why will it be necessary for angels to witness to the earth when the 144,000 and the two witnesses are doing that job? The actions of angels witnessing to the earth are actions which will take place after the 144,000 and the two witnesses to the Nation of Israel have been raptured into heaven and before the 2nd coming. There will be a void time period on earth for witnessing and our Lord will fill that void with witnessing angles. The 1st reaping group is a very sizable group that will live through to the end of the 7 year hour of testing and will enter into the 1000 year millennial reign. This group will be made up of saved persons only.

Those gathered due to the 1st reaping will be saved persons only and will be those who will repopulate the earth during the millennial years.

Rev 14:14 And I saw, and behold, a white cloud; and on the cloud I saw one sitting like unto a son of man, having on his head a golden crown, and in his hand sharp sickle.
Rev 14:15 And another angel came out from the temple, crying with a great voice to him that sat on the cloud, Send forth thy sickle, and reap: for the hour to reap is come; for the harvest of the earth is ripe.
Rev 14:16 And he that sat on the cloud cast his sickle upon the earth; and the earth was reaped.

Note; verse 15 above says the _harvest is ripe_. That denotes the harvest of a good crop, while verse 19 that action gathered the vintage of the earth, _and cast it into the winepress, the great winepress, of the wrath of God_. Therefore, a reaping is seen of the good, which is the saved, and the bad, the unsaved. We should recall the words used by our Lord in Mat 24:22 when He said the great tribulation time period if not shortened no flesh would survive, but, because of the elect that time period would be shortened. The elect spoken of in that verse are the elect of the 1st reaping. We see this elect group in the following scriptures.

Mat 24:30 _and then shall appear the sign of the Son of man in heaven: and then shall all the tribes of the earth mourn, and they shall see the Son of man coming on the clouds of heaven with power and great glory._

Mat 24:31 *And he shall send forth his angels with a great sound of a trumpet, and they shall gather together his elect from the four winds, from one end of heaven to the other.* Again this elect group is seen in the following.

Mar 13:26 *And then shall they see the Son of man coming in clouds with great power and glory.*
Mar 13:27 *And then shall he send forth the angels, and shall gather together his elect from the four winds, from the uttermost part of the earth to the uttermost part of heaven.*

These verses in the past have been pointed to as evidence of a Post Rapture. Clearly what is seen in these scriptures is that the 2nd coming is already in progress. The 2nd coming that will be as lighting travels from east to west will already be in progress when our Lord sends out His angels to gather His elect from the entire world. This action is not a rapture as we are clearly told, that where He is we will also be. Our Lord will no longer be in the present heaven as the 2nd coming will be in progress when the angels are sent out to gather. If the angels were sent before the 2nd coming, a rapture would occur. Yet, that is not what the scriptures tell us. We are told the angels will be sent out after the 2nd coming has taken place.

We should now understand one of the most confused scriptures of the entire Bible. That understanding cannot by yours without understanding the proper placement of chapter 14.

You should now understand why the statement was made, that unless a person understands the proper placement of chapter 14, a person cannot properly understand Revelation.

Chapter 14 verses 17-20

The second reaping of the earth, the second gathering
Chapter 14 is a split chapter;
Those _gathered_ in this reaping will be the unsaved

Verses 17-20 of chapter 14 gives us an account of the 2nd reaping of the earth, the remaining unsaved from the earth. These persons heard the witnessing of the angels listed in verses 6 and 7 and the warning of the angels of verses 8, 9, 10 and 11 but, choose the path of the mark of the beast. The actions of the ones choosing to follow Satan and the beast by taking a mark will have fulfilled the requirement of the unforgiveable sin.

Rev 14:17 Another angel came out from the temple which is in heaven, he also having a sharp sickle.

Rev 14:18 And another angel came out from the altar, he that hath power over fire; and he called with a great voice to him that had the sharp sickle, saying, Send forth thy sharp sickle, and gather the clusters of the vine of the earth; for her grapes are fully ripe.

Rev 14:19 And the angel cast his sickle into the earth, and gathered the vintage of the earth, _**and cast it into the winepress, the great winepress, of the wrath of God.**_

Rev 14:20 And the _**winepress was trodden without the city,**_ and there came out blood from the winepress, even unto the bridles of the horses, as far as a thousand and six hundred furlongs.

Chapter 19 verse 15 pairs with chapter 14 verse 20 telling us a more complete description of what will happen to those involved in the 2nd reaping of the earth.

Rev 19:15 _And out of his mouth proceedeth a sharp sword, that with it he should smite the nations: and he shall rule them with a rod of iron: **and he treadeth the winepress of the fierceness of the wrath of God, the Almighty.**_

Chapter 19 verses 17-21

Chapter 19 a split chapter,
Armageddon, the ten kings that are riding on a promise
200 million man army

Rev 19:17 And I saw an angel standing in the sun; and he cried with a loud voice, saying to all the birds that fly in mid heaven, Come and be a gathered together unto the great supper of God;
Rev 19:18 that ye may eat the flesh of kings, and the flesh of captains, and the flesh of mighty men, and the flesh of horses and of them that sit thereon, and the flesh of all men, both free and bond, and small and great.
Rev 19:19 And I saw the beast, and the kings of the earth, and their armies, gathered together to make war against him that sat upon the horse, and against his army.

At the appointed time God will put in the minds of men over the entire world desires to come into the land of Israel and gather for the battle of Armageddon. By doing so the time of the great tribulation is shortened, as called for in;

Mat 24:22. *And except those days had been shortened, no flesh would have been saved: but for the elect's sake those days shall be shortened.*

Our Lord uses the methods listed in chapter 16 verses 13 and 14 to call the kings of the whole world for His purposes. Part of His purpose was to shorten the great tribulation time period to allow flesh to live, His gathered elect, to live through that time period. He tells in Mat 24:22 that unless that time period is shortened no flesh would survive. In chapter 17 verse 17 our Lord tell us that He controlled the hearts and minds of man to accomplished His desires.

Rev 16:13 And I saw coming out of the mouth of the dragon, and out of the mouth of the beast, and out of the mouth of the false prophet, three unclean spirits, as it were frogs:
Rev 16:14 for they are spirits of demons, working signs; which go forth

unto the kings of the whole world, to gather them together unto the war of the great day of God, the Almighty.

Rev 17:17 For God did put in their hearts to do his mind, and to come to one mind, and to give their kingdom unto the beast, until the words of God should be accomplished.

Rev 19:20 And the beast was taken, and with him the false prophet that wrought the signs in his sight, wherewith he deceived them that had received the mark of the beast and them that worshipped his image: they two were cast alive into the lake of fire that burneth with brimstone:

Those following the beast took hook, line, and sinker, as they were deceived into following the beast. We will see later that those during the millennial reign are not deceived, yet, they follow Satan.

Rev 19:21 and the rest were killed with the sword of him that sat upon the horse, even the sword which came forth out of his mouth: and all the birds were filled with their flesh.

We know there will be a large number killed at the battle of Armageddon, yet, we are not told the exact number. We do know that at least one half of the earth's population will be killed before the battle of Armageddon. Roughly, 3.6 billion persons could still be on earth at the time of Armageddon. That number is based on the 2012 estimate of the world's population of 7.2 billion. We just do not know the size of the saved group that will be gathered during the 1st reaping. We do know they will live through the great tribulation into the 1000 year millennial reign. Those of the 2nd reaping will all be killed. We know that it will take 7 months to bury the dead. As the great tribulation started with a great amount of affection on mankind, so will be the ending of the great tribulation.

Eze 39:11 And it shall come to pass in that day, that I will give unto Gog a place for burial in Israel, the valley of them that pass through on the east of the sea; and it shall stop them that pass through: and there shall they bury Gog and all his multitude; and they shall call it The valley of Hamon-gog.
Eze 39:12 And seven months shall the house of Israel be burying them, that they may cleanse the land.

123

Eze 39:13 Yea, all the people of the land shall bury them; and it shall be to them a renown in the day that I shall be glorified, saith the Lord Jehovah.

Chapter 20

Complete chapter no splitting, yet, explanations are inserted to help with understanding

Rev 20:1 And I saw an angel coming down out of heaven, having the key of the abyss and a great chain in his hand.
Rev 20:2 And he laid hold on the dragon, the old serpent, which is the Devil and Satan, and bound him for a thousand years,
Rev 20:3 and cast him into the abyss, and shut it, and sealed it over him, that he should deceive the nations no more, until the thousand years should be finished: after this he must be loosed for a little time.

Why, will Satan be thrown into a pit and locked away for 1000 years to be loosed at that time instead of throwing him right then and there into the lake of fire as the beast and false prophet were? We saw in chapter 19 verse 20 that those following the beast were deceived. Verses 3 and verse 8 give us that reason. So that he cannot deceive the nations. We have all heard someone say, "the devil made me do it. The claim could be made the beast made me do it. Yet, that claim will lose its validity for 1000 years. Only saved persons will enter the 1000 year reign. Those entering will be the parents of many. Many of those born during the 1000 years reign will not accept our Lord Jesus Christ as their Savior, although they are born of saved persons living in a time that should favor His acceptance. Salvation is a one on one circumstance; no one can stand in for us. The fact that those born during the millennium will be born to saved persons does not mean the offspring will be saved. Therefore, Satan being locked away for 1000 years with no ability to deceive those born, serves to make the point that the problem is not the influence of Satan or the beast or the false prophet, the problem lay within the heart of man, making the wrong chooses. Man not accepting Jesus Christ as their savor for any reason

they claim will have no valid reason when standing before the great white judgment seat. With Satan locked away this is clearly seen.

Chapter 14 verse 1

Our Lord Jesus Christ with the 144,000 on the mount Zion

Chapter 14 verse 1 is a time gap having one time period. That time period is a future time period to the rest of chapter 14. Chapter 14 verses 2-5 which deal with the 144,000 will occur just before the 2nd coming, still in the great tribulation. Chapter 14 verse 1 will take place during the 1000 year millennial reign, after the end of the great tribulation, in the early part of the 1000 year millennial reign. The 144,000 are Jewish persons who have chosen to accept Jesus Christ as their Messiah. They made that choice during the early part of the great tribulation, during the 1st 3-1/2 years. They are the 1st fruits from the Jewish peoples to do so. While chapter 14 verse 1 tells us about an event after the return to earth, please know that verses 2 and 3 tell us about their rapture into heaven after their service of 3-1/2 years likely, witnessing unto the entire world. That rapture of course will happen before the 2nd coming. They will mount white horses and return to earth with our and their Lord Jesus Christ. It is after the return that they will appear on Mt. Zion with our Lord, as depicted in chapter 14 verse 1. Chapter 14 verse 1 has floored many a person. That confusion is brought on by not understanding time gaps. Remember time gaps are not unusual in the Bible.

Rev 14:1 And I saw, and behold, the Lamb standing on the mount Zion, and with him a hundred and forty and four thousand, having his name, and the name of his Father, written on their foreheads.

Listed below in Dan 12:11 we see a time designation of 1290 days. A time designation of 1260 days equals 3-1/2 years, the time of the great tribulation. The listing in Dan 12:11 is thirty days into the 1000 year millennial reign. What is this time period?

125

Dan 12:11 *And from the time that the continual burnt-offering shall be taken away, and the abomination that maketh desolate set up, there shall be a thousand and two hundred and ninety days.*

We should know that there will be built a 3rd Jewish Temple. We should know that the temple will be defiled. We should know this temple is not listed as being destroyed, although we are told in scriptures about the destruction of the 1st and 2nd temples.

The reason we are not told about the destruction of the 3rd temple is because the 3rd temple is not destroyed. This is speculative, but, could explain Dan 12:11 listing a time period thirty days past the 2nd coming. The 3rd temple could be cleansed and rededicated and placed back into service at that time period. This author believes that Dan 12:11 is giving the time period in which the 3rd temple is cleansed and rededicated and placed by into to service and will serve during the 1000 year reign, likely destroyed when this present earth is destroyed. According to the book of Ezekiel, it takes 7 days to dedicate a Jewish temple. Thus three week will be spent in cleansing the defiled 3rd temple.

Ezekiel chapter 43 verses 26 and 27 will be administered, which will rededicate the defiled 3rd temple placing the 3rd temple back into service during the millennial 1000 year reign. It is also believed that is the time period our Lord will reenter the temple with the 1st fruits, the 144,000 listed in chapter 14 verse 1. That group will be guest of honor at the rededication of the cleansed 3rd temple.

Eze 43:26 Seven days shall they make atonement for the altar and purify it; so shall they consecrate it.
Eze 43:27 And when they have accomplished the days, it shall be that upon the eighth day, and forward, the priests shall make your burnt-offerings upon the altar, and your peace-offerings; and I will accept you, saith the Lord Jehovah.

We should understand that the burnt-offerings shall be taken away in the middle of the 7 year time period, which is the hour of testing called out in Revelation chapter 3 verse 10. We should understand that the 2nd coming will occur 1260 days after the events where the burnt-offerings will be taken away. Thus the cleansing and rededication of

126

the temple will take place 30 days after the 2nd coming. Ezekiel chapters 40-48 is thus believed by this earthly author as a description of the 3rd temple to be built during or before the hour of testing the 7 year time period of Dan 9:27. Therefore Ezekiel chapter 40-48 are the blue print of the 3rd temple to be built during the 1st 3-1/2 years of the hour of testing.

The book of Ezekiel has much to say about the great tribulation, the millennial time period and time eternal.

Rev 20:4 And I saw thrones, and they sat upon them, and judgment was given unto them: and I saw the souls of them that had been beheaded for the testimony of Jesus, and for the word of God, and such as worshipped not the beast, neither his image, and received not the mark upon their forehead and upon their hand; and they lived, and reigned with Christ a thousand years
Rev 20:5 The rest of the dead lived not until the thousand years should be finished. This is the first resurrection.
Rev 20:6 Blessed and holy is he that hath part in the first resurrection: over these the second death hath no power; but they shall be priests of God and of Christ, and shall reign with him a thousand years.

What is described in chapter 20 verses 4-6, is a rewards ceremony, a bema ceremony, which was a rewards gathering of the victors of games where rewards for their victories was handed out. Chapter 11 verse 18 of Revelation speaks of this time. No unsaved person will come before this judgment. This is the 1st resurrection over which the 2nd resurrection has no hold. Below Dan 12:12 is listed as that chapter and verse may hold the time happenings, of chapter 20 verses 4-6. If so these events will occur 75 days after the 2nd coming. The words, "blessed is he that waiteth," does not deny our Lord Jesus Christ, and cometh to the blessed events of the rewards ceremony. This seems to be a reasonable span of time; for this event after the 2nd coming, however, this information is speculative and is given as food for thought.

We know that the church group will take part in the activities of chapter 20 verses 4-6 as that information is listed in verse 6. We read, *"**but they shall be priests of God and of Christ, and shall reign with him a thousand years.**"*

Those words are a description of only the church group. Consider the following verses.

Rev 1:6 **_and he made us to be a kingdom, to be priests unto his God and Father;_** to him be the glory and the dominion for ever and ever. Amen Rev 5:10 and **_madest them to be unto our God a kingdom and priests; and they reign upon earth._**

Dan 12:12 *Blessed is he that waiteth, and cometh to the thousand three hundred and five and thirty days.*

Rev 11:18 *[1st]And the nations were wroth, and thy wrath came, [2nd] and [3rd] and the time of the dead to be judged, [2nd] and the time to give their reward to thy servants the prophets, and to the saints, and to them that fear thy name, the small and the great; [3rd] and to destroy them that destroy the earth.*

Chapter 11 verse 18 will occur just before the 2nd coming, yet, is a time gap speaking 1st of a time period just after the 2nd coming, 2nd chapter 20 verses 4-6 and 3rd chapter 20 verses 11-15. Then it says time of the dead to be judged, it is speaking of both the saved dead, which will rise and go before the 1st resurrection, and the unsaved dead, which will rise and go before the great white throne judgment.

Rev 20:7 And when the thousand years are finished, Satan shall be loosed out of his prison,
Rev 20:8 and shall come forth to deceive the nations which are in the four corners of the earth, Gog and Magog, to gather them together to the war: the number of whom is as the sand of the sea.
Rev 20:9 And they went up over the breadth of the earth, and compassed the camp of the saints about, and the beloved city: and fire came down out of heaven, and devoured them.

Although Satan is locked away for 1000 years and cannot deceive any during that time, when he is set free, he has no problem gathering as said like the sands of the sea. Seems it will not take a lot to deceive

those that are willing to be deceived. That is the problem today and has always been the problem.

Many of mankind do not want to follow our Lord and will follow most any who will lead them. This is the separation of the sheep and the goats. Keep in mind the group, like the sands of the sea, will be offspring from saved persons entering into the 1000 years reign from the great tribulation. Seen is three time periods where no unsaved exist upon the face of the earth. At the time of creation before the fall of man, at the beginning of the millennial years, and after the great white throne judgment seat.

These are the only times possible for the fulfillment of the prophecy of Jeremiah 31:31-34; repeated in Hebrews chapter 8 verses 8-12. Why are these times the only times possible? Because of the word *all* contained in that prophecy. God's word is not like the word of man, oh that is good enough, that's the 666 world of man. His words are from His world of 777 perfection. Jeremiah's prophecy could not occur while there are unsaved upon the earth, as all would not accept His commandments.

Rev 20:10 And the devil that deceived them was cast into the lake of fire and brimstone, where are also the beast and the false prophet; and they shall be tormented day and night for ever and ever.
Rev 20:11 And I saw a great white throne, and him that sat upon it, from whose face the earth and the heaven fled away; and there was found no place for them.
Rev 20:12 And I saw the dead, the great and the small, standing before the throne; and books were opened: and another book was opened, which is the book of life: and the dead were judged out of the things which were written in the books, according to their works.
Rev 20:13 And the sea gave up the dead that were in it; and death and Hades gave up the dead that were in them: and they were judged every man according to their works.
Rev 20:14 And death and Hades were cast into the lake of fire. This is the second death, even the lake of fire.
Rev 20:15 And if any was not found written in the book of life, he was cast into the lake of fire.

No saved persons will go before the great white throne judgment set. This is the 2nd resurrection; no rewards will be handed out. All coming before this judgment will be cast into the lake of fire. From this time on no unsaved persons will be upon the face of the earth. This will be the 3rd time that no unsaved will be upon this earth.

Chapter 21

Complete chapter no splitting
A new heaven and a new earth
There will no longer be a temple complex

Rev 21:1 And I saw a **_new heaven_** and a **_new earth_**: for the first heaven and the first earth are passed away; and the sea is no more.

Verse 1 says the first heaven and the first earth are passed away. What does scriptures say about what happens to the old heaven and old earth?

2Pe 3:10 *But the day of the Lord will come as a thief; in the which the heavens shall pass away with a great noise, and the elements shall be dissolved with fervent heat, and the earth and the works that are therein shall be **burned up**.*
2Pe 3:11 *Seeing that these things are thus all to be dissolved, what manner of persons ought ye to be in all holy living and godliness,*
2Pe 3:12 *looking for and earnestly desiring the coming of the day of God, by reason of which the heavens being on fire shall be dissolved, and the elements shall melt with fervent heat?*
2Pe 3:13 *But, according to his promise, we look for **new heavens** and a **new earth**, wherein dwelleth righteousness.*
2Pe 3:14 *Wherefore, beloved, seeing that ye look for these things, give diligence that ye may be found in peace, without spot and blameless in his sight.*

The apostle Peter gives a more detailed account of what will happen, yet, no scriptures go into a real detailed account, as what would be the purpose? Sometimes the advice, "just wait and see," is good advice.

Rev 21:2 And I saw the holy city, new Jerusalem, coming down out of heaven from God, made ready as a bride adorned for her husband. Rev 21:3 And I heard a great voice out of the throne saying, Behold, the tabernacle of God is with men, and he shall dwell with them, and they shall be his peoples, and God himself shall be with them, and be their God:

Rev 21:4 and he shall wipe away every tear from their eyes; and death shall be no more; neither shall there be mourning, nor crying, nor pain, any more: the first things are passed away.

Joh 14:2 *In my Father's house are many mansions; if it were not so, I would have told you; for I go to prepare a place for you.*
Joh 14:3 *And if I go and prepare a place for you, I come again, and will receive you unto myself; that where I am, there ye may be also.*

Will we as the raptured church live in the city of New Jerusalem while it is still in the present heaven? Seems that we will, yet, we can only speculate as no scriptures tell us anything about that subject matter. Yet, likely we do reside in the place our Lord prepare for us as that is what is said in John 14:3. Seemingly, the City of New Jerusalem will be our home in the present heaven and the new heaven.

Rev 21:5 And he that sitteth on the throne said, Behold, I make all things new. And he saith, Write: for these words are faithful and true.
Rev 21:6 And he said unto me, They are come to pass. I am the Alpha and the Omega, the beginning and the end. I will give unto him that is athirst of the fountain of the water of life freely.
Rev 21:7 He that overcometh shall inherit these things; and I will be his God, and he shall be my son.
Rev 21:8 But for the fearful, and unbelieving, and abominable, and murderers, and fornicators, and sorcerers, and idolaters, and all liars, their part shall be in the lake that burneth with fire and brimstone; which is the second death.
Rev 21:9 And there came one of the seven angels who had the seven bowls, who were laden with the seven last plagues; and he spake with me, saying, Come hither, I will show thee the bride, the wife of the Lamb.
Rev 21:10 And he carried me away in the Spirit to a mountain great and high, and showed me the holy city Jerusalem, coming down out of heaven

from God,

Rev 21:11 having the glory of God: her light was like unto a stone most precious, as it were a jasper stone, clear as crystal:

Rev 21:12 having a wall great and high; having twelve gates, and at the gates twelve angels; and names written thereon, which are the names of the twelve tribes of the children of Israel:

Rev 21:13 on the east were three gates; and on the north three gates; and on the south three gates; and on the west three gates.

Rev 21:14 And the wall of the city had twelve foundations, and on them twelve names of the twelve apostles of the Lamb.

Rev 21:15 And he that spake with me had for a measure a golden reed to measure the city, and the gates thereof, and the wall thereof.

Rev 21:16 And the city lieth foursquare, and the length thereof is as great as the breadth: and he measured the city with the reed, twelve thousand furlongs: the length and the breadth and the height thereof are equal.

Rev 21:17 And he measured the wall thereof, a hundred and forty and four cubits, according to the measure of a man, that is, of an angel.

Rev 21:18 And the building of the wall thereof was jasper: and the city was pure gold, like unto pure glass.

Rev 21:19 The foundations of the wall of the city were adorned with all manner of precious stones. The first foundation was jasper; the second, sapphire; the third, chalcedony; the fourth, emerald;

Rev 21:20 the fifth, sardonyx; the sixth, sardius; the seventh, chrysolite; the eighth, beryl; the ninth, topaz; the tenth, chrysoprase; the eleventh, jacinth; the twelfth, amethyst.

Rev 21:21 And the twelve gates were twelve pearls; each one of the several gates was of one pearl: and the street of the city was pure gold, as it were transparent glass.

Rev 21:22 And I saw no temple therein: for the Lord God the Almighty, and the Lamb, are the temple thereof.

In verse 22 we read, "I saw no temple therein," the City New Jerusalem. The following is just for curiosity sake. What happens to the third temple and will there be built a fourth temple? Now of course we have to back up in time to the hour of testing, the 7 years of Dan 9:27. It is clear that a third temple will be constructed. When that construction is started is not clear. Does Dan 8:14 hold a clue as to the starting date of the third temple? This earthly writer does not know for sure. What is the meaning of this scripture? This is the speculative view of the author.

Dan 8:14 He said to me, "For 2,300 evenings and mornings; then the sanctuary will be restored."

Dan 12:11 From the time the daily sacrifice is abolished and the abomination of desolation is set up, there will be 1,290 days.

Previously it was said that the scripture Dan 12:11 could be giving the time of the rededication of the third temple, a time period thirty days into the 1000 year millennial reign. If that were the case then from that time period backing up the beginning of the hour of testing would be 2550 days. That would be the time of the signing of the 7 year covenant agreement. Subtracting 2300 days from 2550 days would leave 250 days. Dividing the 250 days by 30 days for each month, yields 8 and 1/3 month. Following this speculation, that would place the start of the third temple construction in the 9th month of the 1st year after the signing of the covenant agreement.

We know the third temple will be constructed. That is a fact and is not speculation. Certainly, the starting date of the third temple in the 9th month of the 1st year does seem reasonable form the stand point that the temple is finished before the end of the first 3-1/2 years, meaning the construction time would be a little over 2-1/2 years. Dan 8:14 says the temple will be restored. Some contend that what is spoken of in Dan 8:14 is the restoring of the second temple after it was defiled, however, companion scriptures do not support that contention. If the above is what will happen, then of course there will never be built a fourth temple. Some confined that the third temple will be destroyed and a fourth temple will be constructed during the millennial years.

Ezekiel chapter 40-48 reveals details of a Jewish Temple. Is that temple the third or fourth temple? Certainly, if the third temple is restored, then it is reasonable that in Eze 40-48 that is the third temple, yet, if the third temple is destroyed and a fourth built, then what is given is a fourth temple. What do we know from scriptures? The destruction of the first two temples are listed in scriptures as we are told those events would and did take place. Based upon that, it would seem that if the third temple will be destroyed we would be told and giving scripture information about that destruction. Yet, none is given. This writer believes that there will be a third temple constructed, defiled, cleansed, and rededicated. That likely that third temple remains in service throughout the 1000 year millennial reign and is destroyed when this earth is destroyed. We do know there will not be a temple in the new heaven nor the new earth, nor the City New Jerusalem, for God Almighty and the Lamb will be the sanctuary.

Rev 21:23 And the city hath no need of the sun, neither of the moon, to shine upon it: for the glory of God did lighten it, and the lamp thereof is the Lamb.

Rev 21:24 And the nations shall walk amidst the light thereof: and the kings of the earth bring their glory into it.

Rev 21:25 And the gates thereof shall in no wise be shut by day (for there shall be no night there):

Rev 21:26 and they shall bring the glory and the honor of the nations into it:

Rev 21:27 and there shall in no wise enter into it anything unclean, or he that maketh an abomination and a lie: but only they that are written in the Lamb's book of life.

Chapter 22

Complete chapter no splitting
The tree of life the river of living waters
When we've been there 10,000 years it will be like we've just begun

Rev 22:1 And he showed me a river of water of life, bright as crystal, proceeding out of the throne of God and of the Lamb,
Rev 22:2 in the midst of the street thereof. And on this side of the river and on that was the tree of life, bearing twelve manner of fruits, yielding its fruit every month: and the leaves of the tree were for the healing of the nations.
Rev 22:3 And there shall be no curse any more: and the throne of God and of the Lamb shall be therein: and his servants shall serve him;
Rev 22:4 and they shall see his face; and his name shall be on their foreheads.
Rev 22:5 And there shall be night no more; and they need no light of lamp, neither light of sun; for the Lord God shall give them light: and they shall reign for ever and ever.
Rev 22:6 And he said unto me, These words are faithful and true: and the Lord, the God of the spirits of the prophets, sent his angels to show unto his servants the things which must shortly come to pass.
Rev 22:7 And behold, I come quickly. Blessed is he that keepeth the words of the prophecy of this book.
Rev 22:8 And I John am he that heard and saw these things. And when I heard and saw, I fell down to worship before the feet of the angel that showed me these things.
Rev 22:9 And he saith unto me, See thou do it not: I am a fellow-servant with thee and with thy brethren the prophets, and with them that keep the words of this book: worship God.
Rev 22:10 And he saith unto me, Seal not up the words of the prophecy of this book; for the time is at hand.
Rev 22:11 He that is unrighteous, let him do unrighteousness still: and he that is filthy, let him be made filthy still: and he that is righteous, let him do righteousness still: and he that is holy, let him be made holy still.
Rev 22:12 Behold, I come quickly; and my reward is with me, to render to

each man according as his work is.

Rev 22:13 I am the Alpha and the Omega, the first and the last, the beginning and the end.

Rev 22:14 Blessed are they that wash their robes, that they may have the right to come to the tree of life, and may enter in by the gates into the city.

Rev 22:15 Without are the dogs, and the sorcerers, and the fornicators, and the murderers, and the idolaters, and every one that loveth and maketh a lie.

Rev 22:16 I Jesus have sent mine angel to testify unto you these things for the churches. I am the root and the offspring of David, the bright, the morning star.

Rev 22:17 And the Spirit and the bride say, Come. And he that heareth, let him say, Come. And he that is athirst, let him come: he that will, let him take the water of life freely.

Rev 22:18 I testify unto every man that heareth the words of the prophecy of this book, if any man shall add unto them, God shall add unto him the plagues which are written in this book:

Rev 22:19 and if any man shall take away from the words of the book of this prophecy, God shall take away his part from the tree of life, and out of the holy city, which are written in this book.

Rev 22:20 He who testifieth these things saith, Yea: I come quickly. Amen: come, Lord Jesus.

Rev 22:21 The grace of the Lord Jesus be with the saints. Amen.

Most say they are confused by the book of Revelation. Likely, that was your starting point as it was my starting point before the gentle pushing began. My thanks have been conveyed many times to our Lord Jesus Christ for allowing this life changing experience. What was confusion, the book of Revelation, is now purer pleasure to read and with its connections to the rest of our Bible has opened the Bible scriptures and carried this person to new heights in spiritual travels.

Armed with this newly implanted information about the subject Revelation a class was formed teaching others what I have been shown. That has been a real pleasure, however, being aware of what James chapter 3 verse 1 says, "Be not many of you teachers, my brothren, knowing that we shall receive heavier judgment," the knowing exists that what is penned for the consumption of others must toe the line of 777 and not the line of 666, care must be taken.

Now when reading other writings about Revelation, quickly is known whether the writing is worth reading or belongs on the huge pile titled, Man's Creative Mind. Quickly is known whether a sermon or teaching on Revelation is of God or man. Or is a goulash teaching containing a little of both.

May that same experience be yours, and may your confusion have turned to understanding and may your love for His Word continue to grow. May it be that no matter where you are, you simply cannot get His Words out of your mind, and perhaps you too will feel a gentle pushing with His Words placed into your mind. You could be given an assignment to carry out, it does happen.

We look at happening from a lot of different angles. A sincere wish of this earthly author is, "that your perceptive angle allows you to know that the things written are a further revealing given this author. That this author did not find and write through research. That parses for this revealing belongs with our Lord, Jesus Christ.

I had prayed many times over a period of about three months, "what can I do for our church." My wife and I were attending an area church and as with most all conjugations there are many needs. I was recently retired an in failing health. Therefore, I was asking for directions as to what would be a meaningful role that I could serve in. My thoughts along with the prays were that perhaps I could do home repairs for shut-ins, as that was my past. I kept asking yet seemingly no answers came. Then the gentle pushing was felt and my mind flooded with things about Revelation. At first no connection was made between this gentle pushing and the pray being made.

Confusion also occupied my mind as there at first did not seem to be logic to this gentle pushing. Ignoring did not stop the everyday occurrence of the gentle pushing. Then one day a voice saying, "Don this is something you can do." Instantly, I then understood there was a connection between the prays asking what can I do for our church and the gentle pushing. From that time forward writings started with a continuation of things given. Stiff arming was felt from those thinking they would accept. Hibernation seemed necessary for continuance. Now the first of what is hopped will be several writings will be

137

published, with net proceeds' going to our church, to fulfill the pray; what can I do for our church. Like a circle with a starting point of a pray, the circle has now been completed culminating in a pray, that this revealing removes your confusion. That you see the things given could not possibly be the sole work of the author's creative mind. That with those hoped results; you give glory to the heavenly provider, our Lord Jesus Christ. Thank you so much and may our Lord bless you and lead you in the use of information gained.

2Pe 3:18 But grow in the grace and knowledge of our Lord and Saviour Jesus Christ. To him *be* the glory both now and for ever. Amen.

Love His Word   *by*   *Donald E. Morecraft*